# No More Turning Away

## A Revolution in Education
## Solutions for a Violent World

Ronald G. Veronda

*ISBN 0-9709670-0-4*

To Meghan, Lauren, and Matthew

*I may not leave you money or possessions,*
*but maybe I can leave you a little something else.*

**ON THE TURNING AWAY**

*On the turning away*
*From the pale and downtrodden*
*And the words they say*
*Which we won't understand*
*"Don't accept that what's happening*
*Is just a case of others' suffering*
*Or you'll find that you're joining in*
*The turning away"*

*It's a sin that somehow*
*Light is changing to shadow*
*And casting its shroud*
*Over all we have known*
*Unaware how the ranks have grown*
*Driven on by a heart of stone*
*We could find that we're all alone*
*In the dream of the proud*

*On the wings of the night*
*As the daytime is stirring*
*Where the speechless unite*
*In a silent accord*
*Using words you will find are strange*
*And mesmerised as they light the flame*
*Feel the new wind of change*
*On the wings of the night*

*No more turning away*
*From the weak and the weary*
*No more turning away*
*From the coldness inside*
*Just a world that we all must share*
*It's not enough just to stand and stare*
*Is it only a dream that there'll be*
*No more turning away?*

—D. Gilmour and A. Moore, © 1987 Pink Floyd Music Publishers, Inc.

# Contents

# Preface

The beginning is everything. First steps, and the intentions with which they are taken, set the foundation for all that follows. This book had a propitious beginning at the Children's Consulting Center, a "think tank and action center" dedicated to solving the educational and life problems of children. A small group of educators, counselors, teachers, and other dedicated adults gathered to develop solutions to the problems children face today. The Center, supported by the San Mateo/Foster City school district, is located in San Mateo, California.

## Background

In 1993, after decades of work in education, I joined with my dear friend and fellow educator Sandra Larragoiti to do something different to quell the surge of a growing "at-risk" population in our school communities. We weren't exactly sure what that something different might be, but we knew *someone* had to do *something*.

Sandra and I had worked together before. A decade earlier, we teamed with a group of dedicated educators to work with a challenging middle school in San Mateo. I had taught at the school for eight years and was an assistant principal at the time that Sandra joined as a school counselor. We learned to work very closely together with those delightful and needy young teens. The term "at-risk" was new to us then, but the behaviors associated with it were not. Anyone working with teenagers in urban and suburban areas, particularly over the last few decades, must be shocked by the increase in violence, drug use, and gang behavior as well as the more silent demons of depression, bulimia, and suicide.

Our work at the middle school was rewarding. Sharing the immense challenges and responsibilities of the day, with eight hundred teenagers on the periphery of such societal upheaval, created strong bonds between the staff, which last to this day. Our success rate was also quite high. Fewer teens dropped out of school or were arrested as the years progressed, and more were successful in high school. The general atmosphere of the middle school became one of a family. No matter what background or country the kids came from, no matter what war they fled or what physical handicap they were challenged by, everyone was accepted at the school. The issues that these youth were dealing with had little to do with school, but school seemed like the one place the work got done. Many people wondered, "Why does our society wait until teenagers are bursting at the seams before anyone takes action?" That question hit upon the problem and the cause. In the 1970s and 1980s, our society didn't seem to value family, emotions, and life challenges much. No counselors were available in or around schools for young children; such a need was unheard of. It was as if the problems we were dealing with each day weren't seen by the surrounding world.

After years of working with teens, Sandra and I moved to other schools. But in the late 1980s our work paths crossed again as Sandra began to plan a counseling program for young children, ages five to eleven, using newfound grant money. By that time I had become a principal of an elementary school in San Mateo. Sandra and I would often talk about the ease with which problems could be addressed with children, when we didn't wait ten years to begin. It was easy to see, in five-, six-, and seven-year-olds, the beginnings of what I would call today the "recipes" for every kind of problem surfacing later in our society.

When Sandra began what became the Children's Counseling Center in 1987, I was the first principal to sign up. Sandra was free to try innovative counseling approaches with these children and their parents in a center, away from the school setting. That she worked away from school turned out to be significant. She was able to have the "whole child" come to her, with all of life's issues, rather than simply a student with the identity created at school. Never attached to a single school of thought, she used her background in teaching, philosophy, and religion to expand her view and knowledge. Her success with children was quite dramatic. I affectionately called Sandra the Mother Teresa of San Mateo. Her innocence and spiritual presence were obvious to all. She would joke good-naturedly that she was returning spirituality to public education. What many didn't appreciate fully at the time was that she wasn't kidding, and that she was right on target.

While Sandra worked with children and parents in her

office, I worked with some of the same children in school and in their homes, dealing not just with reading and writing but with life issues. We were surprised at how easily we accomplished change using this multipronged approach, and at how much faster we could reach solutions in even the most extreme circumstances.

By 1993, the problems of our society had ratcheted up and were seriously affecting children. Neither of us could stand by and do nothing. Sandra and I sat down and considered the power of our joining forces to create some solutions. We felt that our dualities—man and woman, "yin and yang," counselor and administrator—and our unattachment to current trends gave us a balanced, successful approach. Using our combined experience of working with troubled youth and children for over thirty years, we developed a preliminary proposal to implement our ideas. I would join Sandra at her center, and together we would expand services into other schools and the community. We would seek funding to hire additional staff to not only counsel children and families but also add other creative interventions, parenting classes and teacher training, to more fully meet the needs of the growing at-risk population. We took the plan to Rick Damelio, superintendent of our school district, who had been the principal at the middle school where Sandra and I had first worked together and who was also a dear friend. He understood the commitment and intention we brought to him but answered our request honestly with an all-too-common answer in education today (especially *after* the yearly budget process was completed), "There is no money."

I walked away from this meeting frustrated. I had never bought the idea that money was an antecedent to educating children. In my first year as a teacher, I had driven two hours to pick up reading books discarded from a public school because the private school I was working in had little money for books. I remembered the first time I had been asked to mobilize children to sell candy bars to get enough money for needed school equipment. It didn't feel right in my stomach or my mind. I grudgingly watched this practice grow over a twenty-year period, as the mentality of selling "things" for school funds spread. Hundreds of hours were now spent each year, in nearly every school across the nation, coaxing children and teenagers to sell magazines, pizza, cheap jewelry, and stuffed animals—all to raise money for school necessities. Hundreds of hours were taken away from education, just to make modest purchases of computers or equipment for our communities' schools. These sales events created enormous profits for the salespeople who specialized in school fund-raising. The American way didn't look too American to me. I was blessed and cursed with an ability to see clearly and a conscience that prodded me to do something about what I saw.

After discussing my options with my oldest daughter, Meghan, I resolved to get our project off the ground. I met with Rick the following day and handed him a written request for leave from my principalship; we knew there would be no guarantee I would get my job back. I was determined to find the money and get this work going no matter what. Rick even got tears in his eyes, knowing the chance I was taking. By taking a leave with no guarantee of funding (or a job when I got done), I was risking everything: my principalship, my paycheck, security, retirement, and health coverage, as well as money for food, clothing, and health care benefits for my children. Through my divorce years before, I had already lost nearly all of my possessions and accumulated enormous debt. I had no savings to speak of and lived very frugally. I determined later that the loss of my possessions was in fact a blessing. A large mortgage would have prevented me from even considering this leap.

I believed that our project—founded on Sandra's and my good intentions and our broad professional experience—would be funded quickly. Committing myself full-time to our work turned out to be, in the short run, one of the stupidest decisions of my life. It turned out to be, in the long run, the wisest.

I naively thought that, with the enormous amounts of money available through foundations, someone would quickly pick up and fund our idea of a center to deal with at-risk children. I went to funding libraries that listed sources of grants totaling hundreds of millions of dollars. After dozens of our grant proposals went unanswered, I realized that funding sources would not fund what was different or couldn't be "seen" through the standard pattern of seeing. This failure at grant writing was my first encounter with "paradigm paralysis." People who fund grants, for the most part, want to fund interventions that they are familiar with. But an intervention comes into play only after a problem begins. It creates a repetitive series of reactions to crisis after crisis. If such interventions were working, would we be seeing a massive increase in violence? Our project offered a different approach.

Sandra began the Center with little financial backing. She and her part-time administrative assistant, Joanne Griffin, were paid out of a limited grant. I didn't know that my joining the Center would mean that my income would be nearly nonexistent for one and a half years and reduced drastically for another two years. I nearly went bankrupt and accumulated a debt that will last for decades. (What I also didn't know was that our pay would come in different, and much larger, ways.) But this lack of money became a component of the shift in our way of thinking and the solutions that appeared.

Working for little or no pay gave me a sense of detachment from the established system. This stepping back created a much larger view of what worked and what didn't. It brought nearly every issue of the day to the forefront for examination. I began to question everything. I could often be heard saying, "If I'm not going to be paid, I'm most certainly not going to do what doesn't work." Sandra and I were amazed at how many components did not work.

Rick's trust and support also gave us the freedom to operate in ways that were not merely different but revolutionary. He trusted us enough to leave us alone—something only a confident leader can do. He made sure that the original funding that supported Sandra and Joanne's positions was maintained. We had all heard the cliché that "change is difficult," but to see how far people went to stop change was eye-opening. Rick quieted those who attempted to put a wrench in our works. We would not have survived without his help. Rick stood tall and quietly defended what we began to refer to as the Children's Consulting Center.

Sandra and I set aside everything we had previously been taught was the "system of education." We started over, relying on our extensive working relationships with teachers, principals, parents, and children, taking on any and all problems that children faced. Sandra repeatedly told me, "Pay attention; the children will teach us." Through hundreds of cases, the learning went on. Sandra was right. The solutions we found—by challenging the paradigm that had kept us from seeing—were absolutely astounding.

Sandra and I could not contain our excitement. Actions that have such dramatic effects on children are very motivating. We lived and breathed this new way, learning as much as we could, like eager children. I would often awaken during the night to write down a new idea. The creativity at our Center hit new heights.

The structure with which Sandra and I started—a father figure and a mother figure, a counselor and an administrator, a yin and a yang—was critical to our success. We were able to act with greater compassion and strength. Sandra could model how to listen well, while I was comfortable standing firm when necessary. Sandra easily demonstrated unconditional love, while I tried to establish secure boundaries for children and families. We felt that our society was blatantly missing the roles we took on, and any societal solution had to include their replacement.

Sandra knew that a healthy and successful form of education, one that dealt with education as the pursuit of life, could stop at-risk behaviors from the bottom up. She repeatedly said, "We can't get into every household, but we can get into nearly every classroom." Instead of having an educational system that passes on what society *is*, we sought to create an educational system that could lead society to what it *could be*.

Sandra set up a series of trainings for receptive teachers on what became known as *Innerwork*. These trainings, based on various nonjudgmental processes of self-reflection, unleashed a flood of emotion in teachers and other educators. What started with seven teachers spread by word of mouth over a two-year period to nearly one hundred forty teachers, principals, superintendents, secretaries, and custodians. Sandra sought anyone who might come into contact with children. The sessions opened an arena never tapped before, an arena of inner education comprising childhood issues, dreams, and fears that had been repressed. The learning that took place by all was amazing and appeared to directly benefit the children in the educators' charge. Our visits to classrooms bore this out. So did the teachers' own stories.

## A Community Is Born

The Children's Consulting Center slowly added more committed staff members. Two counselors, Wendy Parker and Kate Nasse, were hired in 1993 and are today senior members of the Center, doing critical counseling work with children, and assisting and training parents and teachers. Margene Janzen joined shortly thereafter, as assistant to Sandra and me, and plays an invaluable role in all aspects of keeping the Center and its true work on track. Joanne Griffin moved on to expand her work in her church and family business. Marti Jacobs joined as a "peacemaker" in 1994, working her magic with a version of conflict resolution that is now utilized in fourteen schools. Valerie Schwarz and Gene Dove, big of heart and spirit, helped me open a creative community day school for middle school–aged children who were suspended or expelled. This one-room school, called Consequences in Life School (CILS), modeled a different way of working with teenagers. Kate McGeary, a master teacher and counselor, took over for Valerie in 1997, and Greg Thornton (setting aside a law degree and taking a significant cut in pay) joined CILS in 1998, taking over for Gene Dove.

Because the Center was so different, with completely new ways of working with children and teens, it attracted many people: teachers, parents, counselors, grandparents, and various other community members. Rosey Blanc, an angel living in the surrounding community, repeatedly came to work with children and teens for free. Larry Hardy and Chris Kindler, experienced substitute teachers in the district, asked to work at CILS whenever a teacher was absent. After some temporary money became available through a violence-prevention grant, Denise Toomer, a licensed marriage and family therapist from the surrounding neighborhood, began working with teenagers out of our office and at school sites. Counseling interns in particular were attracted to the Center because its philosophy could not be found in universities, except in classes taught by Sandra or me. These future therapists were drawn by whispers about a place that worked "differently" with children. Ron Henry, Scott Schaffer, Andrew Costerus, Dea Pierce, and Nicole Huegle trained at the Center and gave of themselves (for the most part without pay) to children in our surrounding communities. Some moved on to other places to continue their work but maintained connections with the Center. One measure of the Center's success is whether people pass on its tools; the work has to spread and cannot be attached to people or places. Then we will create change.

## Where We Are Now

Sandra moved on to continue her spiritual pursuits in Catholic schools, including the College of Notre Dame in Belmont, California, and stays in touch with the Center's staff. Gene Dove offers his work in a multitude of venues, returning at a moment's call to work with teens in serious need. He is a man well aware of his calling.

This unique approach and its astounding success have created a stir, generating calls for consultations, presentations, and work from all over the country. Receptivity to the work that started in San Mateo and Foster City, California, has now spread to other San Francisco Bay Area communities, not by advertising or seeking funds but by simple word of mouth. As an associate professor at California State University Hayward Extension, I taught a class called *Revolution of the Heart* that received nearly the highest rating by attending teachers. I now travel wherever I am called to meet with educators, parents, or anyone who wants to investigate ways of stopping societal violence or enlarging on educational success. As many have heard me say, if you are ready for change—ready to do something different that works—just call, and I will go.

This book is also a way of going.

No More Turning Away

# Introduction

*Using words you will find are strange*
*And mesmerised as they light the flame*
*Feel the new wind of change*
*On the wings of the night*

—D. Gilmour and A. Moore, "On the Turning Away,"
© 1987 Pink Floyd Music Publishers, Inc.

It is time to reverse the decades-long progression of violence and alienation in our society by leading our children and youth "another way": another way that doesn't create the need for locked doors or barred windows. Wouldn't it be heartening if we could reverse this depressing situation where children take refuge in drugs, seek security in gangs, or kill themselves or one another? If we could find a way of raising and educating all of our children more fully? Well, we can.

Pleas for an end to this violence can be heard plaintively from

Moses Lake, Washington
Pearl, Mississippi
West Paducah, Kentucky
Jonesboro, Arkansas
Edinboro, Pennsylvania
Fayetteville, Tennessee
Springfield, Oregon

Richmond, Virginia
Littleton, Colorado
Conyers, Georgia
Santee, California

These towns and cities represent only the most recent and notorious shooting sprees where teens have randomly shot teens, a drop in the ugly bucket of violence that has spilled into every city, county, and state of this country. You may wonder where this violence began and how it has now reached even our youngest citizens.

Yet to someone who has worked with children and teens for over thirty years, the current violence in our society does not come as a surprise. It all makes sense—a horrible kind of sense. These events are the results of a nation increasingly focused more on things than on people; the violence and alienation have been building for decades, if not centuries. If you step back and look, without attachment and without judgment, you can see patterns that show the progression. We can stop the violence by looking at these patterns and by putting into place alternate ways that promote health and happiness.

This book offers solutions to the violence—"another way," if you will. Its approach follows the wise advice of one of the great human beings of our time, Mahatma Gandhi, who said, "If we are to reach real peace in this world, we shall have to begin with the children." He understood that the true education of our children and the attainment of peace go hand in hand. He knew that the best way to stop violence is not to attack its fire but to keep it from igniting in the first place. How do we do this? By raising and educating the next generation differently.

In the news today, along with repeated incidents of teen violence, are reports about our national, state, and local educational systems. Presidents and governors alike are proposing "investments in education," multifaceted plans to reform schools and increase test scores. On the national scene, we hear of referendums on educational systems where billions of dollars will be put forth to improve our schools and education as a whole. At the same time, legislators, educators, and parents are scrambling to understand and to do something about the violence reaching our teens and children. People from Detroit to Seattle and from New York to Florida are voicing their concerns and making determined efforts to change. But these reform measures have one important thing in common: they *will not* and indeed *cannot* be successful.

The reason for this dire prediction has nothing to do with intentions. Surely these caring adults want to create reform and success in school. Surely everyone wants the violence to stop. People's intentions are for the most part good, and the proposed investment of money and time is to be commended. But what most people have not considered is that if we pour billions of dollars and millions of hours into an educational and societal design that is faulty, we move even further away from our goal. Stated simply, it is hard to climb a mountain in a boat.

Those of us who have spent years pursuing answers

to these challenges have learned a number of beginning points critical for change to take place. One of these imperatives is a concept proposed by Albert Einstein, who said, "You cannot create change with the same mind-set that created the problem." This book exemplifies a new mind-set or paradigm that allows true change to occur. By employing this mind-set throughout our schools, we can create a far higher level of learning than previously thought possible, and create societal change at the same time.

By reading this book, you the reader—whether educator, parent, or concerned member of the community—will be introduced to a mind-set where answers to the big questions about life can be found. We will redefine education itself and reexamine fundamental beliefs about learning and children, and the world we have created for them. Much of what is written here will seem revolutionary, but at the same time the assumptions and "facts" presented are common sense, things we all know on some deeper level.

If you are a teacher, you will reconnect to what truly makes education work, things you know intuitively that are not taught in most teacher preparation programs. If you are a parent, you'll be shown how to set aside the trivialities we usually spend so much time on and focus on what has true meaning. The areas of relationships and life that give us the most stress will be examined in a different light.

If you are familiar with the astounding work of Deepak Chopra, you'll notice that the concept of the "bigger picture" matches his "second attention," where we move back, distancing ourselves from the material reality or the things that first grab our attention. In moving to the bigger picture, we will also be doing what Gary Zukav recommended in his book *The Seat of the Soul*—using a multisensory approach to education and life rather than solely that of the five senses. For those of you who have been intrigued by the writings of Erich Fromm, you'll recognize the shift recommended here as one from a consciousness of "having" to one of "being."

This book is presented in two parts. Part 1 is composed of the theory behind the paradigm shift, and Part 2 explores how we can apply this different and wiser mind-set. Throughout the book, names and minor biographical details have been changed to honor children's and teenagers' privacy. In a few cases, composites have been created to further protect identities.

In Chapters 1 and 2, we will explore the concept of paradigm and how to move beyond the current mind-set for true, systemic change. We will look and laugh at our own "paradigm paralysis," uncovering basic areas for change that are often blocked from our consciousness. In Chapter 3 we will redefine education, challenge basic tenets of educational theory, and consider the classroom as the ground for social change.

Chapter 4 introduces and explains the theory behind the "bigger picture" and the Wisdom Paradigm. To be healthy, happy, and fulfilled as individuals or as a society, we must fully explore all four realms of our humanity: the material, psychological, emotional, and spiritual (body, mind, heart, and spirit). To assist us in this examination, we will critically examine the limited mind-set currently in place in the Western industrial world, a mind-set that I call the *bodymi*. This filtered way of experiencing the world focuses heavily on the material world of the body, and includes only the physical portion of the mind—the brain. In other words, it is a way of living in the body and a limited part of the mind while excluding the other realms basic to our humanity. We will look at how denying any one realm, let alone two and a half realms, can cause personal illness or societal violence. The problems of our society today stem from this massive denial. We will demonstrate how to stop this violence and destruction by reopening all four aspects of our lives.

In Chapter 5 we will look at the importance of both an inner pursuit and an outer pursuit in education. The concept that *all learning begins within you* will be set as a foundation for the educational design. We will also explore the power of nonjudgment. Since any form of judgment in the educational process impedes learning, we must seek to be nonjudgmental at all times.

The second half of the book suggests ways we can apply the theoretical suppositions. Chapter 6 brings us back to where all of the answers and the "new" design can be seen clearly—in the kindergartner. Miracle and perfection are evident in every child at this young age. To work effectively as teachers, to be nurturing parents, to be healthy and happy human beings, we must do what the kindergartner does—live life fully, and explore the *order* that is within us and around us, not the *disorder* we seem to see when we look at life in an incomplete way.

Problem solving is critical for change to take place. In Chapter 7 we will move away from the limited, reactive way of dealing with problems so prevalent in our society today. If we are to create true solutions, we must see problems fully. Then we will note how easily we can explore, develop, and put into action *solutions* to problems—no matter how large they are and no matter how long they have been with us. We will even examine how important fear, pain, and stress are to problem solving. In this chapter we will also explore a lifelong tool that everyone has access to—the power of metaphor.

Wouldn't it be nice to know what qualities master teachers share that make them so successful? In Chapter 8 we will identify and discuss those qualities. Here again our findings make sense, but you might be surprised to realize these "universals" have little to do with our society's current concepts of education.

We cannot leave a discussion of education without addressing the epidemic that has come to be called attention deficit disorder. We will look at this "disease" in Chapter 9 through different eyes, seeking order where before there was the appearance of disorder. Solutions to these behaviors and problems are presented throughout the book, but, again, they come from places we usually don't look.

In Chapter 10 we will look at how adults can help model

change for the child or teen. One family member, or one outside elder, can have a dramatic impact on a whole family.

In Chapter 11 we will discuss what a new "classroom" might look like. We will offer specific suggestions for teachers to change their own classrooms and for principals or superintendents to begin the gentle shift from the Knowledge Paradigm of the past to the Wisdom Paradigm of the future. These suggestions will aid anyone who is part of the greater educational community. And since education is a process, not a finite search for single answers, plenty of room will still be left for everyone to creatively explore their own answers.

In closing, the Conclusion is a bullet-by-bullet restatement of the key points covered in these chapters. It is offered as a source for those who wish to embrace the philosophy inherent in this book. It will also serve as a list to remind us of what composes another and wiser way—a way that will help us all guarantee that in the future there will be no more turning away.

PART 1

# A Foundation for Change

# 1 The Importance of Paradigms

*The real voyage of discovery consists not in seeking new landscapes but in having new eyes.* —Marcel Proust

Thomas Kuhn, in his book *The Structure of Scientific Revolutions,* challenged scientists to be aware of what he called paradigms. These paradigms, Kuhn explained, were mental models or patterns of thinking that shaped how scientists thought, felt, and acted. He said, "To look at these paradigms is to look at a filter for one's own perceptions." No matter how objective scientists might wish to be, their paradigms influenced their interpretations.

To think of how a paradigm works, imagine you are holding a three-foot piece of window screen around your head. Into this screen is cut a pattern of holes of different sizes and shapes that determines to a large degree what you see and what you don't. This screen is your paradigm, and nearly every member of a society is handed a screen with the same design. Now imagine that thoughts, ideas, and events have particular patterns or shapes. As they come to you, only some make it through your screen—those that correspond to your societal group's pattern of thinking. Those of shapes not recognized by your society are blocked. Anything foreign to your paradigm cannot make it through.

A person growing up in an indigenous tribe in a rain forest will not see the world in the same way as an Englishman from Cambridge. One is not better than the other; they simply see through different screens, each to his or her advantage according to surroundings and circumstances. If those circumstances change—the tribesman goes to live in London or the Englishman now must survive in the rain forest—the previous paradigm will not work. Hence a revolution of thought will undoubtedly result.

The same holds true at broader levels. If in a family, a society, or even a business, something no longer works well, the underlying mind-set, or paradigm, needs examining. Denise Breton and Christopher Largent, in *The Paradigm Conspiracy,* state that a paradigm reaches a crisis when it doesn't solve problems the way it once did. At that point, people are called on to move outside the paradigm for solutions. Old liners in power then declare that change is not needed. Fearful that the existing order may be challenged, they vehemently propose, "We just need to work harder at making what we have work better." Breton and Largent point out how this stance most often triggers a revolutionary response.

The word *paradigm* has been used and abused since Thomas Kuhn first coined it. What are cited today as examples of "paradigm shift" more often than not are examples of a change of wrapping rather than an entirely different "gift." A gasoline-powered automobile with a newer, larger engine is not a shift of paradigm over previous gasoline-powered cars; it is just a better model of the same thing. The computer, however, is a dramatic shift of paradigm over the calculator or the word processor. Paradigm shift is always dramatic.

One of my favorite examples of paradigm shifts is Joel Barker's story of the quartz watch taken from his and Ray Christenson's popular video, *The Business of Paradigms.* He mentions how some Swiss watchmakers went to their higher-ups with a new kind of watch. Since the Swiss had been premier clock makers for hundreds of years, they had a particular way of thinking, a paradigm, that described what a clock or a watch should be. This new watch (called a quartz watch) didn't have all the springs and gears of a "Swiss watch," so the higher-ups disdainfully dismissed their own watchmakers. A short while later, the spurned watchmakers went to a clock convention and set up a table to demonstrate their invention. Two groups of watchmaking entrepreneurs representing Seiko and Texas Instruments were not paralyzed by the "Swiss watch" paradigm. They saw that these men had invented an entirely different concept of watch and snatched up the patents. In a matter of only a few years, the Swiss watch industry—the royalty of the world's watchmakers—was nearly dead, a victim of a lack of understanding of a paradigm shift. As Barker says, "When the paradigm shifts, everything goes back to zero."

Reality is reality!

Since the beginning of time we have known that the world is flat. Simply look around you. You can see from horizon to horizon. It's obvious. It's a fact. Anyone who thinks differently is a fool. Don't pay attention to them.

We know the world is round. Science has proven it. It's been known for hundreds of years. You can sail one way around the world and return another. It's a fact. Anyone who thinks differently is a fool. Don't pay attention to them.

After sending satellites and orbiters out into space, we can now prove the world is actually oblong. It's a fact. We have photographed it and we can measure it. Everyone knows this. Anyone who thinks differently is a fool. Don't pay any attention to them.

Physicists know the world is nothing like what it looks like. It's actually composed of atoms that are 99.9 percent empty space. The rest is pulsating energy. What you see is an illusion of matter. It can be proven. It's a fact. Anyone who thinks differently is a fool. Don't pay any attention to them.

We now know the world is ... ●

Another example of a paradigm shift is the development of atomic submarines. As late as the 1950s and early 1960s, diesel submarines were still in use. These antiquated submersibles were limited in range, couldn't stay under nearly as long as they needed to, were relatively noisy, and gave off an oil residue that caused enemy ships and planes to see them. These shortcomings endangered all on board the submarines as well as the sailors on the ships the submarines were to protect. Since diesel submarines didn't fulfill their original mission of staying hidden and protecting ships, the submarine paradigm was challenged. The atomic submarine, designed with a new energy source and a performance level far beyond what was previously conceived as possible, was the result. When the *Nautilus* traveled totally submerged to the North Pole, the world was stunned. The submarine later broke all undersea speed and distance records. Nevertheless, the "old salts" stayed with the diesels—in the best of cases, retiring from the navy, and in the worst, going down with an outdated boat. The new breed of submariner, able to transcend paradigm, became an elite lot.

The paradigm presented in this book is not a new watch or a sophisticated submarine, but an entirely different way of seeing education, and the world. The Wisdom Paradigm proposed here might be called the quartz watch of humanity.

# 2 Paradigm Paralysis

*You have to be careful if you don't know where you're going, because you might not get there.* —Yogi Berra

Most of us at times have trouble seeing what's right in front of our faces. Joel Barker calls this phenomenon "paradigm paralysis." This paralysis results from everyone having been taught to see (and not see) in the same way. By filtering what we see, we can ignore or deny what we don't want to see. What we exclude falls in the "paralysis" realm. (The expression "can't see the forest for the trees" refers to this interesting phenomenon.) We may feel foolish when we finally see something previously unseen because it is sitting right in front of us.

## The Material World

Paradigm paralysis is apparent at many levels. Our current societal paradigm, which focuses on the material world and which defines our "selves" as our bodies, emphasizes what we can see, measure, or prove. We inherit this paradigm and pass it on to the next generation without most of us ever being aware of its existence. It underlies the structure of our schools, saturates our political system, and permeates our economic system. It has let us reach the ends of the earth and the foothills of space. It has allowed us to create a scientific revolution and move quickly to mind-bending industrial and technological discoveries. It has also done more. We as a society have not looked deeply at its shadow side. In the shadow, inside the paralysis, lies the problem and therefore the ground for change. By denying huge amounts of information from the world around us, we set ourselves up for major difficulties. It is like walking down the sidewalk focusing on the cement squares, and not looking at the parking meters, lampposts, and cars crossing through the intersections. It is just a matter of time before a crisis occurs. We tend to address problems only after they have become big enough to demand our attention through pain, threat, or even death. Such crises force us to see the shadow and give us the opportunity to do something about the underlying problems. If our desire to do something is deep enough and we seek true solutions, we can change the paradigm itself.

Richard Tarnas, philosopher and teacher probably best known for his comprehensive work, *The Passion of the Western Mind,* has lectured at length about the modern and postmodern eras and the shadow side of the current paradigm. He speaks eloquently about the trade-off of the scientific age, pointing out that we made great discoveries for science, but at an enormous cost—the cost that comes from ignoring the greater mystery of life, the world beyond the material. One comment in particular stayed with me: "We have taken our need for individual freedom and moved past the point of balance to a degree that can only be described as pathological."

To satisfy our selfish wants, which we house under the banner of individual rights, we now ignore even the needs of our own children, the elderly, and the infirm, a sure sign of societal ill health. In this society, we step over men and women lying on the sidewalk and ignore the cries of teenagers who are so lost and alienated that they want to kill their families, their friends, and themselves. Those of us in the industrialized world have allowed our bodies and our own needs to dominate issues of the heart, the welfare of others, and the mysterious world of the psyche and spirit.

## Making Work Our Life

Our society's emphasis on the material world is evident in our definition of the word *work*. Today, work refers to what you do to earn a living. We can trace that concept back to industrialization. At a position on the assembly line, you're not concerned about where the items you work on come from or where they go. You work at your singular task unattached to reasons for making the product and uninterested in the final product itself. In essence, you are performing a task for money alone. Your view is limited, and deep ideas and creativity have no place. Arthur Zajonc, physics professor and author, presented some tantalizing views on the relationship between the industrial age and the work world in Richard Tarnas's class at the California Institute of Integral Studies. Dr. Zajonc stated that in 1801, the craft tradition ended. People no longer saw work as art, or a family trade worthy of pride. That may not sound like much, but he pointed out the enormity of the event. He told of how Eli Whitney demonstrated to President John Adams and Thomas Jefferson the amazing invention of interchangeable musket parts. For the first time, it was possible to take gun parts, mix them up, pull them out at random, and put them together into workable rifles. This opened the door for mass production.

Not too many years after Eli Whitney, Frederick Winslow Taylor instituted the concept of scientific management. To manage "scientifically" meant to use your intellect and the scientific method to set up your factory for the greatest efficiency. Taylor's ideas on efficiency, when applied, brought massive monetary gain. As you might expect, many industrialists then strove to make industry as efficient—and thus as profitable—as possible. A secondary result was that individual creativity, personal pride, and the sense of community were removed from the workplace. Taylor surely did not envision that his ideas would spawn a "head-without-heart" approach to work, but that is what happened.

Henry Ford later extended Taylor's ideas into the formation of the first assembly line. Workers no longer needed to be fully skilled. They were put on the production line, which in the end mechanized humans themselves. Building was no longer a craft but an efficient means of making larger quantities of products at an increased profit.

Previously, when a craftsman was making a piece of furniture, for example, he might rise early and begin work before the heat of the day, and work until he finished a major portion of the piece, feeling satisfied, stopping where he might naturally pause. His schedule was not arbitrarily determined by a clock. He might also work late into the day, without objection, to finish a cabinet. The finished piece would be art, as well as trade-ware. It was something he took pride in and finished with his signature.

On an assembly line, a worker's every move was studied and made more efficient. He sanded furniture legs all day or operated a lathe that did one type of cut. The worker might do that one procedure well, but the end piece did not belong to the individual to sign or take pride in. Work became boring and senseless, its value reduced to the pay it would bring. Doing such a task all day, for set hours, came to be called a job. Set hours, the nine-to-five seen as normal today, became known as the workday. These new concepts were not received well by the populace, and in fact were rebelled against, to the point of rioting. The mechanized process didn't feel healthy or right. Jobs and the workday replaced esteem and meaning with efficiency and money. This reduced positive cooperative relationships and in their place promoted competition and opposition. The previously coveted relationships of apprentice, journeyman, and master were almost totally phased out. The sense of community provided by guilds was replaced by the antagonistic relationship of unions and management. The purpose of work was reduced to simply the earning of money. Money was no longer a tool of commerce or a tool to assist a person in pursuing life dreams, but an end in and of itself.

What started with Eli Whitney is still going on today. Work as merely a means to earn money is now the norm. Preparing for work and acquiring money have become the focus of our entire lives. We all know the saying about the misplaced importance of work: no one on their deathbed wishes they had worked more. Yet look around. Are we stupid? No. We're paradigm paralyzed.

### A Limited View of Education

The industrial age contributed as well to our society's current paradigm of education. Our present educational design was built on the premise that learning is a factor of the brain alone, and it is structured so that children of different ages are taught separate curriculums while they are housed together in "classrooms." Teaching in this paradigm is from teacher to student, with the teacher judging each child's success. The purpose of education, in this design, is to prepare students for the workforce. This design was an offshoot of the industrial revolution, and as such, it served the industrial world well. It prepared masses of people to work on assembly lines at segmented tasks, removed from the whole. It emphasized the pursuit of a job over the pursuit of an individual's life, and helped reinforce the age-old belief that money is an end rather than a tool to an end. The system legitimized what became the teaching of curriculums over the teaching of children.

We don't hear much today about the many educators, philosophers, and thinkers such as John Dewey, Jiddu Krishnamurti, Rudolph Steiner, Albert Einstein, and Erich Fromm, who were seriously concerned about the limited mind-set being taught in our schools. These scholars warned that life, much less education (which should be the preparation for life), is too important to shrink into just the pursuit of a job or money. Krishnamurti stated it clearly: "If we are being educated merely to achieve distinction, to get a better job, to be more efficient, to have wider domination over others, then our lives will be shallow and empty." John Gardner, former Secretary of Health, Education, and Welfare, said frankly, "I am certain that twenty years from now, we will look back at education as it is practiced in most schools today and wonder that we could have tolerated anything so primitive."

The day-to-day practice of education, though perhaps not primitive, has many examples of paradigm paralysis—paradigms within the basic paradigm, you might say. Here I'll cite only a few.

Middle school and high school teachers normally have 130 to 150 students per day. The students are brought through in shifts, 30 at a time, and are taught a single subject at a time. As an educator, I know this is not how learning takes place. But these "shifts" fit the assembly-line concept underlying our industrial-age paradigm, so sometimes even our least successful practices never reach the level of consciousness needed to create change. The only imitation of change that occurs at these schools is changing the schedule, maybe the length of the classes or the class rotation—an example of what I referred to earlier as changing the wrapping but not the gift. Such action substitutes for real change.

I'll never forget a parent conference I conducted while working as a middle school teacher. Back-to-School Night, generally held after the first few weeks of school, is usually not the time for a parent/teacher conference, but I was concerned about a particular young teen, and her mother had approached me, away from other parents. As I began informing her of my concerns, her eyes became serious and her jaw set. She was obviously upset. After what seemed like twenty minutes (but was certainly only five), the mother stopped me to ask a clarifying question about her daughter. Further conversation made me realize, to my horror, that I was talking about someone else's child. I had so many kids I didn't even know their names yet! I felt foolish, and the mother, while certainly initially relieved, must have wondered who, for goodness' sake, was teaching her child.

Another example of paradigm paralysis: all across this country, millions of pubescent teens are taught in like-age groupings in classrooms. We are housing that kind of hormonal energy in four walls and calling it a school? Anyone would have to have his or her head examined to do this in the first place, let alone continue the practice for more than a hundred years.

Paradigm paralysis exists when it comes to learning itself. Imagine collecting all of the assignments you were ever given in school, from kindergarten through high school and beyond. Imagine compiling every lesson and lecture, the essays, the reports, the final exams. If your imagination is even slightly good, you must have an image of a mountain of paper. Reenvision all the check marks, the red circles, and the all-important grades. Oh, and don't forget the state testing used for important decisions that affected not only your personal progress but also that of your teachers and schools.

How large a container would you need to house all of this? Maybe a large warehouse?

And how many theorems and bits of information are housed in this warehouse? How many single facts were you tested on to see if you learned them?

Now comes the critical question: How much of that information is still with you today? I've asked this question of hundreds if not thousands of parents and educators. Some people giggle or fidget, and some look toward the ceiling and then back at me with embarrassment. Many laugh and say, "How about a box full?" The answer usually boils down to a somewhat disgusted "Not much."

Much of what we sent to the "forgotten warehouse" we may have "learned" at some point, but not for long. We learned things to pass an exam or to please a parent or teacher, but what we memorized for those reasons we forgot a few months—if not a few days—later. Even if you were considered a good student or consistently got good grades, it's a decent bet that you let go of more than you kept.

Consider, for example, learning a foreign language. How many of us took three, four, or even five years of a foreign language only to remember a few cute expressions, or the swear words learned outside of class? How many of us only learned how to say hello or how to order a few dishes in a restaurant? Why? The answer is actually simple. Learning begins with the desire to learn something for life. This key point is not part of our current paradigm of education.

Please do not misunderstand. All of us did learn a significant amount in school and would continue to with the system we have. The trouble is that many of us learned almost in spite of the current educational system. It's time to study what really promotes effective learning and alter the educational design accordingly.

# 3 True Education

*Education is not merely acquiring knowledge, gathering and correlating facts; it is to see the significance of life as a whole.* —Jiddu Krishnamurti

Some educational processes are successful and some are not. To understand why this is so, we need to look at the definition of education itself.

*Educare*, the Latin predecessor to the English word "educate," comes from the same root as *educe*, which means "to bring out." Teaching, then, should be a process of bringing out, not putting in. Yet our educational system is built on the premise that educators/teachers/adults put in data. They determine what is to be learned, how it will be learned, and how the success of this teaching will be measured. This is backwards on all points. The system for the most part ignores the learner, who should be the beginning and the prime focus of all educational steps.

An experienced educator knows that students must be *hooked* for a lesson to be successful. This hooking is an internal process for the learner; it is different from what we do externally and call motivation. Hooking connects with a desire in the learner, rather than simply fulfilling an adult's expectation or a curricular requirement.

I can recall many times years ago when, as a teacher, I would plan my classes according to an outline someone else created, far removed from me or my students. I would get enthused about a particular event in history and thoroughly prepare lessons for the 150 middle schoolers assigned to me. For the most part, I would give them all the same lessons, though I tried hard to adjust my approach according to students' needs. I loved history, I loved teaching, and I loved teenagers, so I was at a distinct advantage in my attempts to pass on the key points of each lesson. If you are an adult today, this is probably how you were taught history, as well as most other subjects.

After preparing a lesson for days, I would come to school excited about teaching. I would try to make the lesson relevant to current events and to make it entertaining by using overhead projectors, music, and story-telling techniques. (Computers weren't available then, so CD-ROMs were out.) I would let the hidden actor in me come out to enliven the presentation and pull the students into activities to "learn for themselves." I was sure most students left the classroom with a whole lot more information than when they came in, but by the end of the semester, I was often discouraged to find they didn't remember much. They may have humored me with their attention, they might show some success on a test if it was given shortly after the lesson it pertained to, but by June, how much did they still remember? We teachers would laugh about those days of well-prepared lessons that students didn't respond to, though they were more frequent than we would have liked.

Sometimes the opposite would happen. I would come in quite unprepared for the day's lesson and then "wing it" by chasing after an interest of the students that day. These impromptu lessons usually had something to do with life and weren't on the state's outline. Sometimes the lessons I prepared for the most were the least successful, and sometimes the ones I prepared for the least, students told me later, would be remembered forever. Why was that? Success or failure was determined by whose desire was at the heart of the lesson. In the first instance, *I* had the desire; I probably learned a lot in teaching the lesson. In the "winging it" example, the desire came from the students. Their learning began with their desire.

## Critiquing the Current Design

Let's consider more closely our current educational design, and then step back to look at it again from outside the paralysis of paradigm. Then we'll make some basic shifts and examine another, more effective way.

Currently, our philosophy of education begins with a number of basic premises: all children learn the same way; they progress through their education by age, year by year; learning is a function of the brain; and education (teaching) is performed from teacher to student. We provide basically the same information to all children (what we have been told they are to learn) and assess how well they can give back this information from memory. We grade students on how well they perform this process and use grades to motivate them.

. Keep in mind the concept of paradigm paralysis introduced in Chapter 1. We inherit paradigms. Initially, at least, we do not choose them. Paradigms are designs that form over years to match certain desires or beliefs of a society. Sometimes when the society changes, the design does not. The pressure caused by the paradigm not working well eventually causes dissatisfaction, if not alienation, and massive change occurs. True change happens with a shift of basic beliefs—a paradigm shift.

Remember, immediately before change occurs, paradigms look silly or foolish. Our purpose here is not to make people look foolish. In fact, educators who are able to find success in an outdated design should be especially proud of their work. Earlier, I used the analogy that we in education are trying to climb a mountain in a boat, the boat being the design we have been given to use. We should laud educators who make such amazing progress with millions of children today. They actually *are* climbing the mountain while being forced to carry the boat of society's paradigm. This is an exhausting, and in some ways thankless, job, especially in a finger-pointing society. Many, if not most, educators are heroes who have taken on the most important job in the world. They are helping to form human lives in a society that little values that pursuit.

Let's look at the first premise of the design we inherited: all children learn the same way. We know better than that. In every classroom and school, some children fit the learning design well, some sort of fit, and some do not fit at all. We accept this because that is the way it has been. But people are not objects on an assembly line. Each of us is beautifully unique. And trying to fit multiple-shaped pegs into round holes hurts, causing alienation in the short term and depression or violence in the long term. We see this in our children and youth, and in society as a whole.

With our linear way of thinking (a direct result of our paradigm), we can't get past a simple numerical way of grouping. Setting up classrooms or teaching groups by age or grade levels is superficial and ineffective, but it is part of the design we were handed, so even though we know better, we continue to ride it like a dead horse. There is a huge variance—a delightful variance—among six-year-olds, or eighty-year-olds. Let's appreciate and use this difference instead of trying to squash it. We can group children by similar interests or dreams. Or better yet, let's set up families of cross-age learners. Older children thrive when given responsibilities with younger children; younger children thrive when put under the tutelage of an older child. Of course there are always exceptions to this. You need to match carefully according to each child's desire and needs. Don't fall back into the assumption that everyone does the same thing. That's the factory mentality. Within limits, we can allow children to choose their projects and assist them by teaching tools (curriculums) to use in their pursuit. This method pulls *out* of the child and has *desire* inherent in the choice. Internal desire promotes learning, whereas external motivation is a hit-or-miss proposition.

We also know better than to believe that learning is a function of the brain. The brain is the storage bank and the nervous system the transferer of thoughts; neither is the thinker. People are not just organs and tissue. We are much, much more than that. Ignoring a person's desires and dreams does not make sense. The greatest block to cognitive learning is an emotional need that has not been recognized, acknowledged, or addressed. Not addressing emotions guarantees less academic growth. Do you want to increase test scores in a school? Don't focus entirely, or even initially, on the brain! Focus on life and heart issues, and then dive into the cognitive process and the accompanying academics. Test scores will go off the chart.

Another fallacy of the current design related to this point is that we learn *outside in,* from teacher to student. In fact, people learn *inside out,* from internal desire outward to other sources. This one premise makes our current system unworkable.

According to Benjamin Bloom's Taxonomy, our current educational system focuses on knowledge recall. In most cases, the teacher gives out factual knowledge; the learners take in the knowledge and then give it back to the teacher, demonstrating that they have absorbed the learning. According to Bloom, this is level one, the lowest level of learning. The subsequent levels of this cognitive domain are comprehension, application, analysis, synthesis, and, finally, evaluation—and these six levels represent only one domain. (He also added two more entire domains of learning—the affective and psychomotor, which for the most part are ignored entirely by our educational design.) Forty years ago, Bloom found that 95 percent of test questions in schools were at level one. Some movement on this front has been made over the last two decades, but improvement is not advancing to the degree we might expect. Adopting different ways of doing things isn't part of our paradigm.

Grading is also a stalwart part of our current structure. Although we are never happy with how it makes us feel, we continue to grade—to judge—our children. We change the symbols used to judge, but not the concept itself. We ignore that for some people grading actually *stops* motivation. Why do we do things that we know inhibit learning? Paradigm paralysis.

One other key point of the current paradigm looks silly, if not sad, from the outside. Our educational design puts the responsibility for learning on the child. If the educational system, which was designed by someone else, doesn't work, and the child is unsuccessful, we consider it the child's fault.

Because our basic design has never worked exceptionally well, many educators have searched for an alternative. What we call "special education" became the prime alternative. The problem is that in setting up the structure, we failed to heed Einstein's advice. We tried to make change without changing the mind-set that originally caused the problem. In fact, we even enlarged the most problematic concept, judgment, to one of disability. Declaring a child disabled is a pretty huge judgment. We've now come to realize that our children are not disabled; the design of education we inherited is disabled. If judgment stops learning, huge judgment stops it hugely. A common expression of teenagers today is "Stop 'dis'ing me!" As Jean-Jacques

*Consequences in Life School helped me in millions of ways. It showed me to respect people and to help people. They showed me how to write in a journal and to forgive people and that people will forgive you. CILS was very fun and it showed me how to get along with people, so I did. At the school we helped the kids next door and it was fun so I did it. At my old school I had lots of cuts. But when I got to Consequences in Life School, I never cut because I liked it very much and because the teachers were so nice.* —**A.**

Rousseau declared, "The children will teach us, and they will not be satisfied with half truths." I believe the following truths are known by all of us on some level: Every child is a genius. Every child, regardless of physical or mental states, no matter how challenging or limited he or she appears, is a miracle of life. If we begin here, we will progress faster and farther than if we begin with limitation. Remember, "The beginning is everything." Begin with limitation and your results will be limited. Begin with the miracle that is your child and your results will be miraculous. All education should be special, because all children are special.

## The Myth of the Three Rs

Reading, writing, and arithmetic are the meat and potatoes of our current educational system. They are the flags of measurement we always raise when we look at education. This is ironic. Reading, writing, and arithmetic are not "education" at all. They are the *tools* for education, tools to be used in the pursuit of something else. As a society, we have forgotten the something else.

This something else is a person's life dreams and life itself. It is understanding who you are and what the world is all about. It is the greater context that we call the *bigger picture*. As teachers, we were trained to teach curriculums separately rather than children in their totality. The three Rs are critical tools, and curriculums are supportive components of our current learning design. But by teaching reading, writing, and arithmetic out of the context of students' lives, we have never been able to attain our desired level of success or performance.

Have you ever wondered why school districts purchase new curriculums every four years or so? Is it to feed a multi-billion-dollar industry? Is it because the teaching of a curriculum, rather than the teaching of a child, is an incomplete approach?

Whenever you pursue something and are off target, the pursuit is never-ending. Have you ever been driving to a particular destination but were unknowingly on the wrong road? If you are as stubborn as many of us are, you may have refused to question your original assumptions about the way. You may have found yourself driving faster and faster, as time passed, more determined than before, not daring to question the direction itself.

Many years ago, when I was first beginning to challenge how we approach learning, I sent out an e-mail request to all of the schools in the district's network. I asked anyone who had a minute to send me the names of any reading programs they could remember purchasing or teaching over the last ten or fifteen years. A number of colleagues responded, and I soon had a list that covered a standard page in three columns. It included such titles as Semantic Mapping, Initial Teaching Alphabet, Neurological Impress, and Diagnostic Prescriptive Approach.

I typed up the list, put it on an overhead, and took it to a presentation I was giving a few nights later. I covered up the overhead and then line by line slowly uncovered all of the titles. As I did, I read them out loud, one after the other. It took only a few minutes, but it seemed like forever.

I then asked, "Are we stupid?"

After a pause, I said, "I personally don't believe we are. Then how come we keep buying different programs to teach the same basic thing and we keep getting the same limited results? Do you realize how many millions of hours and billions of dollars are spent seeking, evaluating, purchasing, and selling these programs to teachers and parents each year? You'd think we would simply get good at what we do and repeat the process."

I then quoted Michelle Karns, a delightful speaker and educational activist, "You will never teach children to read with a curriculum, but you will never fail to teach children to read when they are in a relationship with an adult who truly wishes them to read." People and relationships, not things, make education work.

As a young teacher, I always believed that "a good

*CILS for me was not a punishment. It was a wonderful experience. My teachers gave me love and hope. The children we helped, a couple classes down, made me feel as though I was going for others and not just me. Their smiles and laughs could make me forget any tough situation. Mr. Dove, no matter what, always showed patience with my mood swings. He taught me patience and love for humanity. Mrs. McGeary taught me that the past is the past and look forward to the future. She made my future positive. If I had not gone there, I would have never learned the meaning of life. Thanks to CILS I will always shine and look for the bright side.* —**V.**

teacher can teach anything!" I might word that a little differently today, but I still believe it. I'm not saying that we should throw out curriculums. What I am saying is that if we keep focusing on the curriculum as the object of teaching, we are going to keep having the same limited results. One of my favorite Einstein quotes is "Insanity is doing the same thing over and over and expecting different results."

### A Common-Sense Design

Now let's look at a different way. Let's consider a philosophy of education that says that millions of children learn in different ways, are interested in different things, and need to get ready for different lives. Each child's needs and interests determine what is taught and how it is taught. The teacher and parents find out what the child loves, what he or she is strong at, and then use this information to move the child into lessons to help prepare for the life he or she longs for. Strategy will change plenty of times along the way. If attempts to teach the child are not successful, the teacher will adjust the approach to suit the child. Adjustment will continue until the child is again successful. The child, with the teacher's help, will accumulate examples of his or her activities and accomplishments. Projects demonstrating the child's progress will be proudly displayed, and the adulation the child receives will be a prime motivator.

In this newer design, the child's dreams and needs are never forgotten or displaced, because that is where all education begins. If, as a teacher, I can tap into that lifestream, I will be successful.

By adopting the material motivations of the industrialized world, we have been pulled away from the understanding held by philosophers and teachers that all learning begins within. People as diverse as New York City's former Teacher of the Year John Gatto, endocrinologist and philosopher Deepak Chopra, and professor and author Parker Palmer emphasize that learning takes place from an intrinsic desire.

No desire on the student's part means no sustained

learning. Is the student's wish just to get a good grade or please a parent? If so, the learning will be retained only for the time it takes to do that, and then it will be "released" or forgotten. Learning that does not relate to the student's life will be released to make room for things that are connected to the student's desires.

All learning begins with the learner—not with the teacher, and not with the curriculum. It doesn't matter whether the learner is a child, a teenager, or an eighty-year-old; the learning process is the same. This simple philosophy may appear obvious, but when it is fully understood and practiced, it can dramatically increase a teacher's effectiveness.

I am not suggesting here that students determine what goes on in the classroom. Rather, I am saying strategies exist that allow learning to *begin with the student*. We can implement this philosophy of education without throwing out our entire educational structure. But such a change will necessitate a major shift in how we approach education and the learner. When you as teacher, parent, or concerned citizen have finished this book, you will more than likely have much to question about our school system. Change can be made smoothly. In fact, it is already taking place.

At our Children's Consulting Center, and elsewhere throughout the country, small groups of educators are creating a revolution in education within the existing system. The successes are dramatic, successes that have come from working with some of the most challenging students in the most difficult circumstances. At the heart of this revolution is the belief that education should be true to the root of the word. We as educators should strive to bring out the strengths and desires of every student. From that base we can all learn more of the depth and breadth of human experience.

# 4 The Four Realms of Being

*I have no doubt whatever that most people live, whether physically, intellectually, or morally, in a very restricted circle of their potential being. They make use of a very small portion of their possible consciousness ... much like the man who, out of his whole body organism, should get into a habit of using and moving only his little finger.... We all have reservoirs of life to draw upon, of which we do not dream!* —William James

Each of us has a *body*, a *mind*, a *heart*, and something mysterious we call a *spirit* or *soul*. Since some people are uncomfortable with the term *spirit*, I also call the spiritual aspect the *bigger picture*. These four realms correspond to the physical, psychological, emotional, and spiritual parts of being human. Each is a paradigm, because you can "see" and think differently in each arena. The realms are separate and yet interrelated.

We can see these four components fully interacting in children at play. Young children eagerly awaken to their bodies, running and twirling at ease. They actively engage their minds, asking questions a mile a minute. They laugh and cry and seek friendship and love. They dream and fantasize about being moms and dads, superheroes and the household cat. Their mouths fall open and they stare in awe at soap bubbles, butterflies, and rainbows. The four realms spin around and within one another in complete balance. Our adult world freely allows young children to explore all four realms. Not only is exploration allowed, it is a cause for delight. We wouldn't think of stopping what is so natural and delightful and life affirming.

Imagine these four realms in a circle that the child freely explores, moving from one to another in perfect flow. The circle is like our circulatory system with its natural fluidity and balance, pulsing round and round. Now imagine if, after a few years of this freedom, one of these areas were blocked. What would happen? Can you see how this obstruction would cause an energy blockage, just like a clogged artery?

What if a child were no longer free to express or experience his or her body? What if he or she weren't permitted to run, dance, or play?

What if a child's mind were stifled? What if his or her inquisitiveness were suppressed?

What about the heart? What would a child's life be like without love? What if he or she could no longer laugh or cry or know friendship? What if a child were told that expressing emotion is a weakness?

And the spirit. What would happen if a child were not allowed to talk about dreams? What if he or she were to lose the sense of awe?

You probably know an adult whose life has been stopped up in one of these areas. Maybe you know someone who is ashamed of his or her body and is hiding the shame behind inches of fat or oversized garments. You undoubtedly know someone who has been called stupid and now shies away from any challenging intellectual task. Maybe you know a man who has been taught that expressing emotion is weak or not masculine. Those of us who work with children have certainly seen these things, and much more. In fact, if we look carefully, we can even note when these constrictions begin and how they grow.

It's easy to see how catastrophic a blockage of any area would be to that dancing, laughing, dreaming child we thought of earlier. When the flow of life is stifled, unhappiness—perhaps illness—soon follows. As that child gets older, we might attribute the child's imbalance to a defect of birth, instead of seeing it as a natural progression, and part of a recipe of societal ill health.

Let's go back to the child racing freely through the four life realms. We all can relate to that magic and delight because we have experienced it ourselves; if you have children, you see it there in front of you in full splendor.

For the most part, these four regions are still honored in kindergarten, even in a formal school system. As Robert Fulghum says in his famous essay "All I Really Need to Know I Learned in Kindergarten," you learn to "live a balanced life. Learn some and think some and draw and paint and sing and dance and play and work every day some."

But we treat kindergarten, and kindergartners, differently. From first grade on, our educational design shifts. A wall comes down, isolating the world of the body along with the brain, the physical organ of the mind. Emphasis moves to the physical world and cognitive processing. For ease of description, I call this region the *bodymi* and the pattern of thought that corresponds to it the Bodymi or Knowledge Paradigm.

The poor first-grade teacher is faced with the daunting responsibility of leaving what is so well received by children—namely kindergarten—and introducing "learning" as our society sees it. Now it is time to learn how to sit in your seat, wait your turn, stand in line patiently, and "fit in." Children must learn to read and write. Now the curriculums arrive. Metaphorically, and literally, the door of the classroom shuts.

Emotions are downplayed, and dreaming is no longer considered a positive pastime. Dancing and singing, for the most part, stop. Drawing, painting, and other artistic endeavors are scheduled in regular intervals as rest or entertainment. Their value becomes secondary to the learning of reading, writing, and arithmetic. Playing is now relegated to a fifteen-minute recess in the morning and a thirty-minute break following lunch. Fantasy is considered wasteful.

Intelligence, in this mind-set, is perceived as a factor of the body's brain, something we are born with. In the material realm, intelligence is measured—and judged. The concept of failure now enters the child's world in full force.

If the child *fails,* he or she will be held back. Repeating a grade becomes the greatest judgment of all. Our current paradigm of education is based on this system.

A very critical wall now gets erected between the *bodymi* region and the remainder of the mind, heart, and spirit. In this paradigm—the Knowledge Paradigm, housed in the *bodymi* realm—the "physical" brain is considered the center of learning. Only the logical and factual world is kept within the walls. By perceiving the world in this manner (without being conscious of it), we seal off nearly two and a half regions of our humanity.

Remember the warning above, about closing *one* area? What we have now done, systemically, is close two and a half realms of life. And they are the biggest realms of all. If shutting down one realm causes illness, what does blocking two and a half realms cause? What does that do over five to ten years? What happens to a society that follows this pattern of raising and educating children for decades, if not centuries? A massive societal coronary is waiting to blow.

Let's explore these realms and their paradigms in more depth to understand and enjoy the differences between them. We can then use this new understanding to devise some solutions.

### The Body

First let's look at the body, or the physical and material consciousness. This is the primary level, the surface of the four realms. It is you in your body and the world that surrounds you. It is the world of the five senses, discussed in depth by Gary Zukav in *The Seat of the Soul.* This world is composed primarily of what we can see, touch, smell, feel, and hear. This is the world that we get up to each morning and the world that we experience step by step through the day. It is the world of mortality, clearly defined by our physical beginning and ending. We learn to cherish birth, and more than likely we are taught to fear death. The finite realm is considered "real." Since this reality can be seen or not seen, touched or not touched, its foundation is a black-and-white duality.

In this reality, everything is explained as it relates to the body. The thinking and seeing that go on seem to be in our heads, so we identify them with the brain. The brain, we are taught, is where we store knowledge, which is composed primarily of facts. Even our emotions, which are harder to describe or identify, are given an organ of origin —the heart. Though we know emotions are not really related to this critical pumping organ, that assignation is part of the body paradigm, so we do not question it.

In the material world of the body, we are taught not to focus on what might come before the obvious arrival of the body. What happens after death is also of little importance. Something out of order within the body is called diseased; the body's ease has been disturbed. In this paradigm, disease affects only the body, so changing some aspect of the body is the way to cure it. We cure illness primarily by changing the chemistry of the body or by adding or subtracting a body part. Genetics and microscopic DNA are the beginning and the end-all; they represent the mystery of the body paradigm.

## The Mind

The mind represents the vast psychological world. For our purposes, we will consider the mind to be composed of two parts. The first part comprises the brain and the nervous system, the physical organs we associate with the mind. This is the astounding computer/file cabinet where we store our knowledge and its delivery vehicle, which transmits the brain's impulses. The second part of the mind is the nonphysical portion, which is more nebulous and mysterious and probably more critical. To this part we ascribe insight, intuition, and other psychic processes. By distinguishing these two sections of the mind, we acknowledge that the physical mind is a conduit for the nonphysical energy associated with thoughts, knowledge, and life.

Psychologists and medical professionals somewhat acknowledge this distinction by explaining that we probably use only a small portion of the brain. The part we "use" falls under the physical description above. The mysterious portion, far less understood and less provable, is where our dreams are pictured. It is also the place that many cultures call "magical." In this critical juncture, the spirit joins the body.

## The Heart

When we think of heart, we think of emotions, a realm less readily measured than the body. I have heard our emotional world described as an ocean, its constant ebb and flow underlying all that we do. For thousands of years we have created poetry, drama, and music to try to illuminate this realm. Here begins the world of the verb, of movement and change. In this world we have pain, fear, joy, and love. The virtues lie here as well. The heart is a nebulous realm. Those who do not set emotions aside are considered the creative ones, the artistic ones, the Maya Angelous and Michelangelos.

Anthony Robbins, author, inspirational speaker, and successful businessman, stresses in his presentations just how important emotions are to our lives and to our society. He points out how all of us want to feel good, how emotions underlie all that we do. Even negative emotions, the most painful emotions, "may be our best friends." If we heed these signals and use them to motivate change, they become the "ultimate power." He notes the obvious connection of emotions to such astounding events as the procreation of children and the start of war.

No decision in life is made without an emotion, or a denial of emotion, to spark it. By staying in contact with our emotions and giving them appropriate expression, we can literally direct our lives. Denying the importance of emotions on a personal or societal level is an invitation to disaster.

## The Spirit/Bigger Picture

The fourth paradigm is that of the spirit, or bigger picture. From this universe, all other paradigms—the body, mind, and heart—are thought to emanate. Buddhists and Hin-

A newspaper reporter called me for a phone interview, having heard stories from principals and teachers of this "different" place. She wasn't really sure what we did at the Center; she just knew we had a different educational approach and strategies that relieved stress. I invited her to come sit with me, knowing that I would have trouble explaining a different paradigm of education in ten minutes over the phone, but she was on a deadline. I took a chance and decided to pull out of her the answers she sought over the phone.

I could hear stress in her voice (most likely due to the deadline she had mentioned).

"Why did you become a reporter?" I asked.

She answered that she was just working at this job to help pay the bills, implying she had a greater dream. So I asked, "Do you love writing?" I suspected that she did.

There was a pause, and then a quiet "Yes."

I then asked, "What is it that you truly want to do? Do you want to be the best newspaper reporter in the world, or do you long to be a poet? Do you want to write a great novel, or maybe create short stories or plays? What is your dream?"

Again there was a pause, indicating to me I was shifting her into a deeper part of herself. She answered firmly but from a long way off, "I want to write a novel."

I then said, "Paula," using her first name for the first time, "imagine you came to sit with me, and spent an hour getting focused and jazzed about actually starting your novel today. And imagine that later in the evening, as a result of our talk, you actually spent two or three hours beginning your book. How would that make you feel? Would your head be a little higher going to work tomorrow? Would you smile throughout the day?

"When you went back to your job and were again confronted with some of the things that give you stress, wouldn't you see these irritations differently? Might you even laugh? How would your day go with your coworkers? How about with your husband or boyfriend?"

There was a long pause on the other end of the phone. "So this is what you do with children and teenagers?"

"Yes," I replied, "this is the first step." I waited a moment or two and then added, "And when life again feels good, don't you think you'd be motivated to work even longer on your book?" ●

dus call this realm "the part between our thoughts" or "the speaker of our thoughts." In this realm, the spirit tells the mind, which in turn instructs the body. The spirit is bigger than words, so silence is common. Intelligence is everywhere, swirling as energy through everything about us. Some call the spirit world "nature's intelligence."

The spirit contains the immensity within us and the immensity outside of us. A philosopher or sage would describe it as where we come from and where we go. Many religious texts describe the spirit as the part that cannot be born and the part that cannot die. A Hindu mystic demonstrates clearly its preeminence in the four realms:

*If you have not realized your body's potential,*
*you have not missed much.*
*If you have not realized your mind's potential,*
*you have missed little.*
*If you have not realized your heart's potential,*
*you have missed much.*
*If you have not realized your soul's potential,*
*you have missed all.*

—*Adi Shankara* (sacred Hindu text)

## The Power of Four

Since all four realms of body, mind, heart, and spirit are critical to the human experience, a balance of them must exist for a person to fully explore the human adventure. Most of us probably feel most comfortable in one or two realms, and we have a tendency to "see" in the manner of those realms. Knowing all four ways of seeing the world can help us understand others as well as ourselves. To be truly balanced, we must be awake in our bodies, stimulated in our minds, aware of feelings and intuitions, and in contact with the larger world.

As stated earlier, if any one realm is shut off for a significant length of time, then ill health in one or all of the four realms will certainly follow. The body shows physical symptoms (what our society looks for and most responds to). The heart fills with pain, the mind becomes confused, and the spirit—the most important of all—is "lost." In extreme instances, all four "illnesses" appear.

Our society, which today operates primarily in the one-and-a-half region I call the *bodymi*, exhibits many of these signs. After hundreds of years of living in this limited way, we have become so unhealthy that physical illness is rampant, mental illness is frighteningly increasing, our emotional world is severely out of balance, and some of us have lost our humanity, our souls. Our technological discoveries are almost beyond imagination, but our singular focus erases the importance of feelings and ignores humanity in the bargain. We have denied our children their life dreams, their creative and emotional expression. Only teens with no concept of the greater picture of life could commit the murders we have seen recently in the news.

Though we have paid a tremendous price, there is still time to learn, and time to create true health. We need only

**no more turning away**

For thousands of years before the time of Christ, a symbol that represented evil appeared in writings. This symbol was a simple hand gesture with the fingers projected from a closed fist. It was a warning of a false life—the literal translation being "All you see is all there is." This "false life" doesn't sound evil until you think carefully. The people of that time were being warned not to be open only to what is obvious. They were being reminded that there is more to life than what can be known through the senses—things like love, compassion, and the mystery of life. An acorn is so much more than the obvious brown shell and bitter nut inside—it has the potential of a living, majestic oak tree.

Believing only in what we can see, touch, feel, hear, or "prove" is very limiting. Today a physicist might argue quite convincingly

to refocus on all four regions of our humanity, paying particular attention to the heart and spirit. This can be done in a systematic and natural way.

One way to guarantee that all four realms find full expression in our educational system is to reverse the order of their implementation. Currently we begin in the body realm, considered level one, and then proceed to level two, the mind, and stop midway. Instead, I have teachers start in the fourth realm and move backwards. They begin in the spiritual paradigm, staying long enough to "hook" the child's life desire. Then they move to the heart, makthat the physical world is actually an illusion. We are all made of atoms—energy and empty space. The world is not just the material one we see. In fact, thinking in this limited manner can be downright dangerous. If all we see is all there is, then we can make a quick assumption that we come from nowhere and we go nowhere. Life just is and then it isn't.

How dangerous can this way of thinking be? Read the news. The two teens that killed at Columbine believed just this: they could kill and die, and that was all there was. Much of the horror and violence of today is a direct result of that limited view of life. Heart and spirit are excluded from the mind-set "All you see is all there is." A heartless and soulless world most certainly would be evil. ●

ing sure to deal with underlying emotional issues that might block the lesser cognitive processing that will follow. It is important to stay away from the *bodymi* realm at the start, because that is where the concept of "failure" resides.

After establishing the realms of spirit and heart, teachers (and parents, or any concerned adults) then enter the realms of mind and body. By using this design, we are no longer constricted by the order of the four realms. We can move freely from one to another, as long as all four are regularly tapped.

## Working with the Four Realms: An Example

How does this design actually work with an individual child? I received a call from an associate superintendent informing me that a fourteen-year-old named Sylvia was having serious difficulty in her middle school, and more than likely would be expelled. She had struck another girl on the way home from school and had threatened the girl and her mother. This was not the first time Sylvia had been abusive. She had a record of severe verbal abuse to teachers, principals, parents, and even strangers.

I'll never forget the morning Sylvia arrived at our office with her aunt. She was cussing out her aunt like a seasoned sailor. I noted her powerful presence, her anger, and the fact that her aunt, not her parents, had brought her. I didn't judge; I just paid attention.

I invited Sylvia, her aunt, one of our teachers, and an interpreter into a conference room. Sylvia's aunt only spoke Tagalog, one of the languages of the Philippines. The room could hold six to seven people comfortably, but it wasn't big enough for Sylvia's anger. We settled into our seats. I talked to Sylvia, not to the adults present. I didn't begin by asking her about her offense, her classes, or her discipline record. I asked her about her life. I politely acknowledged her aunt and asked Sylvia where her father was. She quickly answered, "He's dead!" I paused, noting her pain, and also her anger. I expressed my sorrow for her loss and then asked, "Where is your mother?"

Sylvia responded with venomous disgust, "She left when I was two!" I sat with this news in silence, trying to imagine how it feels to be abandoned by your mother and then have your father die. Sylvia had just shown me the "sense" of her anger. There, I knew, was where solutions lay.

I apologized to Sylvia's aunt and asked if I could have some time alone with Sylvia. I then asked all of the adults to please leave the room. My trusty friend and mentor, Madison, stayed with me. He is my cocker spaniel/guru—blind, deaf, happy, and always loving. He helps me establish a relationship quicker than any psychiatrist could ever dream of.

I reminded Sylvia that I was a school principal, not a counselor or psychologist, and that my job was very different from what she might think. She smirked. And then I began—very differently from the way a principal might be expected to begin.

"Sylvia, I don't care about your grades. I don't care about your classes, your homework, or, at this time, school at all. I'm not here representing your principal, your teachers, the superintendent, or the courts. I don't care about your reading or your math. In fact, let's set those things aside over here. They are only this big." I showed her a tiny opening between my forefinger and thumb and motioned to a little box sitting next to me.

Sylvia stared at me, probably wondering who this weird person was.

Then I said, "I want to talk about something much more important than these things. I want to talk about *you*." I paused.

"Tell me your story. What happened to your parents? Tell me all about it."

Sylvia looked at me suspiciously.

Madison came to my rescue by cuddling up to Sylvia's leg. Slowly Sylvia began to open up and tell me about her life. Her mother left when she was two, and no one knew where she went. They heard she was living on the streets in Oakland. Her father was killed when Sylvia was only seven years old. He had been everything to her. Since Sylvia was the only one in the house who spoke English, she took the phone call from the emergency room of the county hospital the night her father died. The emergency room nurse, not knowing how old Sylvia was or who she was, told her that a man (her father) who had died had this phone number and address on him. She explained that he had been stabbed several times; they thought it was drug related. Sylvia, a seven-year-old girl whose mother had left her, took this call.

When Sylvia told me this, her eyes filled with tears, and I could see the seven-year-old sitting before me. I started crying with her. I just sat there with Sylvia, and cried.

I learned later that her aunt was scared to be living in this country and spent nearly all of the day and night in her own world, trying to deny the violence surrounding her. She loved Sylvia dearly, and had raised her for the last seven years, but in her attempt to love and protect her, she never talked about the losses and the pain. Neither did anyone else.

A child suffering fear, loss, and death had never dealt with the biggest issues of her life in any significant manner. Is it any wonder that she was angry? Plenty of people had probably dealt with Sylvia's anger or the results thereof, judging her behavior "bad," but I wondered how many people had tried to teach her reading or mathematics without ever dealing with the deeper issues of her heart.

To make a long story short, Sylvia was relieved to tell her story and have someone—an adult male principal, no less—stop what they were doing to listen to her. She became curious about the Children's Consulting Center and the Consequences in Life School. After more conversation, involving all of the other concerned people, Sylvia asked if she could come to our school. We took her in, and the teachers began the long task of reenergizing her life and dreams.

Sylvia bloomed quickly. I didn't know it that first day, but Sylvia had beautiful dimples. They showed up regularly at CILS. We all commented, of course, which made her blush. After hearing her dreams, and dealing directly with her emotions, we found out that she loved mathematics. Sylvia delighted in the daily mathematics work, which built her esteem and enabled her to do the other work that interested her less. By the time she left CILS, she was studying calculus.

The work Sylvia needed to do, and the challenge to the

teachers, was great. She got angry on many occasions, one time stomping her way across the city to get home. We had plenty of opportunity to show her how to redirect her anger into leadership, art, and writing.

Sylvia was on probation because of her previous collisions with the law. The evening after she stomped home, she got picked up by her probation officer and taken to juvenile hall, because of a miscommunication between the school and her probation officer. Her temper flared. Many people would have left her there to cool off for the weekend, if not longer. But I wanted to show her not only that we cared for her but also that we would protect her, from anyone or anything. That is a critical point with children and teens; much of the violence arising in teens today stems from issues of security. Getting Sylvia out of the hall was difficult, especially on a Friday evening, but it was more than worth it. The drive home from the detention center was filled with important conversation and important silences, the sure sign of a spiritual connection. She never forgot what I did for her.

Sylvia graduated from CILS five months later. How did she do it? Through forming and nurturing relationships, the adults at CILS addressed the essential parts of Sylvia's life before anything else. Her emotions were allowed healthy expression, and we were fully available for *her* needs, not ours. After her spiritual and heart realms were opened, she was then free to delve into her dreams (where she wanted to go in life), her mind (curriculums), and her body (dance and sports).

Our strategy of working backwards through the four realms is fairly consistent; we vary it slightly according to the life needs and dreams of each child. Students at CILS begin their "education" by dealing with some personal aspect of the bigger picture: their dreams, their life story. Any emotions that might block learning are brought to the surface, the first step toward resolution. Nothing in this ocean of emotion is ignored. Academics are then fully explored to prepare students for return to a regular school and adulthood. They are now free to work on their studies because their larger problems have been acknowledged, if not addressed. Academically, the results are nearly always astounding.

The format of moving from spirit to heart to mind to body has miraculous results—not with some children but with all children. As an educator, I get excited by that. As a father and a human being, I take from it much hope.

# 5 Education Outside and Education Inside

*The Master said, "If there is one thing in this world that must never be forgotten; if you were to forget everything else but were not to forget this, there would be no cause to worry. While if you remembered, performed, and attended to everything but this one thing, you would in fact have done nothing whatsoever.*

*"It is as if a king sent you to a country to carry out a task. You go to the country, you perform a hundred other tasks, but if you have not performed the task you were sent for, it is as if you have performed nothing at all."* —Rumi

If we asked a hundred children why they go to school, how do you think they would answer? It certainly depends on how old they are, but a typical answer might be "To learn to read and write" or "To get smart." Some might tell you they want to be a doctor or a baseball player. A teenager might respond, "Because I have to."

What would you think if they answered by saying they wanted to prepare for life? Or, stranger yet, if they replied,

"To figure out what all this is around me" or "To find out who I am"?

This may sound startling, but education *is* the preparation for life. It is the pursuit of understanding who we are and what the world is. To live fully, we must "walk" in both directions, inside and outside ourselves. To have a healthy society—to stop the all-too-common violence, alienation, and hopelessness—we as individuals and we as a community must explore both ways.

Our world is so vast it boggles the mind. From the top of a mountain or from the highest skyscraper, the view seems endless. Whether we lose ourselves in a poem, chase the precise order in a calculus equation, or overhear the grateful ruminations of someone just glad to be alive, we can't help but be humbled by the world's complexity and simplicity, its chaos and order. Learning about the world is an endless, wonderful journey.

### The Dash in Between

One aspect of learning about the world is learning to truly appreciate the time we spend in it. In 1999 I traveled back to Borgiallo, Italy, the village my family emigrated from just after the turn of the century. No member of my immediate family had ever returned there. I went hoping to reconnect with family, but at the very least I wanted to reconnect spiritually with the country of my forebears. Though my father had said he never wanted to go to Italy, I knew differently. I think he hesitated because he had lost much of his ability to speak his native language. (Ironically, the Alzheimer's disease that finally took him first fully returned his ability to speak Piedmontese, the dialect of his birth.) I promised him before he died that I would return for him. With the birth of my son a half year after my father's death, the time seemed right—the circle of one hundred years somehow complete.

From dust we come and to dust we will go. So teaches the Judeo-Christian tradition that many of us grew up with. Tombstones, crypts, and mausoleums are our way to commemorate the dead. I spent hours looking through village cemeteries for my family name. I took pictures of the sites and of the small portraits left on many of the headstones of people most likely related to me. Sometimes the tombstones contained short statements of family, beauty, and spirit, but what predominated were two numbers—the date of birth and the date of death.

It makes sense to commemorate both birth and death, but the incompleteness of this tradition struck me that day. As a society, we pay little attention to what comes before that date of birth and, most certainly, even less attention to what might come after. But the point that really stood out for me—an exclamation point to the incompleteness of our mind-set—is how seldom we acknowledge the importance of "the dash in between."

I remembered a couple lines of a poem I had once heard that went something like "It matters not how much we own: the cars, the house, the cash. What matters most is how we live and love and how we spend our dash." The "dash," of course, is our life. One way to motivate lost teenagers or parents is to have them reconnect with what is important in life. A common approach that works well is asking questions that lead our consciousness back to the important things we have buried, the things that go beyond the insignificant things that we spend so much time chasing—like jobs, money, and possessions. "When you die, how do you want to be remembered?" or "If you were to die tomorrow, what is there that you haven't done? What is there that you haven't said?"

Few of us know when we are going to die. A man seventy years old may live twenty-five more years, while a youth of sixteen may die in a car crash by nightfall. Regardless of how old we are or what our life circumstances are, the task is the same—start living fully, aware of what is truly important. Wouldn't it be heartening to have no regrets at the end, so that what is written by our actions remains long after we are gone?

My dear friend and colleague Sandra always amazed me with her gentle and humble wisdom. She would say something to me very matter-of-factly and it would take a moment for what she said to penetrate. Invariably, my mouth would fall open at her insight.

Sometime in 1993, shortly after we had started what would become the Children's Consulting Center, Sandra and I were sitting around trying to figure out strategies to use with our "at-risk" children, when she said, "You know, it is quite easy to know what is important in life."

I thought to myself, "You've got to be kidding. Haven't we as the human race spent thousands of years looking for the answer to that question? People spend lifetimes looking, paying therapists and teachers, going through books, and you say it is easy!"

Sandra continued, "All you have to do is look at what is important to a very young child, and then look at what is important to a person on their deathbed. Aren't they the same things?"

My jaw dropped.

"The task," Sandra concluded, "is to keep those things in focus during the time in between."

## Another Way of Looking

Let's take a different step toward understanding who we are and what the world is. In our scientific paradigm, we see children as growing bodies. Our thinking of life as a physical reality creates a finite and linear mind-set. We only acknowledge what we can see, touch, or prove. We pay less attention to the child in the womb because the embryo is outside of this paradigm and outside of our view. But after children are born, we eagerly watch them grow. We see every new step or look as a progressive development. A child mimicking simple words or recognizing colors gives us delight. Recognition of a number or a simple intellectual concept is a hallmark for celebration. We also assume in our linear mind-set that we gain knowledge as we get older. But are you aware that in many cultures life is perceived differently?

Mexico is not as industrially developed as the United

States, so it is not uncommon for people here to think it a simple country with simple people. But Mexico has a rich spiritual history, and those who speak Spanish and other Latin languages better express than we can in English the passions of the heart and spirit.

In Mexico I once heard a phrase that really gave me pause. A mother was staring at her newborn baby with love in her eyes, but also with deep respect and honoring. What she gently said to her baby I translated as his being "closer to God." I paused, thought for a minute, and then it hit me like a ton of bricks. I realized the mother was commenting on the baby in a spiritual perspective and how much closer the child was to God, having just left where we all come from. As I talked to her about the phrase, it made perfect sense to me, since I had some understanding of her culture. She assumed that just after birth and just before death we are in a more advanced state. Her words reflected an entirely different way of seeing birth, a view that encompassed more than a simple physical reality. She was acknowledging that the child had come from a place bigger than that which we see and touch. Having just entered this temporary physical world, the baby was more knowledgeable, more spiritual, rather than less knowledgeable and in need of development. To the Mexican mother, her child's eyes mirrored the awe of spirit so recently in the presence of God. If *the beginning is everything,* then isn't this awe toward the child a good place to begin? By beginning with the miracle, the results can be miraculous. By beginning in the temporary and the material alone, as we do currently in our culture, the results are temporary and limited to the physical surface of life.

## Inner Knowledge

The journey inward is just as vast as the journey outward. But in our society it seems we have spent our time learning about *things* and how to duplicate or consume them and have forgotten who we are and why we are here. As a quote I read recently says, "We have been taught to love things and use people instead of love people and use things." The advancement of civilization has a shadow side. Author Daniel Quinn is not alone in thinking we actually have been going backwards for thousands of years. While technological advances have reached levels never imagined before, they are trite when compared to the meaning of life itself. We don't think of the achievements in computer technology on our deathbed. Though the computer may very well be an essential tool for advancing our life and even societal consciousness through unbridled communication, technology is still a tool.

Today we thirst for more knowledge than our narrow paradigm promotes. Whether we drink from spirituality, art, music, dance, or tai chi, the thirst is the same. We are seeking wholeness—in particular, a reconnecting of heart and spirit. As Matthew Fox points out in *The Reinvention of Work*, "In bringing together outer and inner work, we are contributing to a cosmology, a making whole, a putting of order into our lives and that of our species."

I had the delight and pleasure of working with Yvonne and Rich St. John-Dutra, the creative founders of Challenge Associates, at a number of their Next Step trainings. At this particular one, a number of teenagers were participating who had been filmed with Challenge Associates on a "Teen Files" documentary. After working with Rich and Yvonne, these teens were comfortable doing intense and personal work. As I was introducing the audience of counselors, teachers, trainers, parents, and teens to the Wisdom Paradigm, I took a chance and used teenagers to demonstrate techniques firsthand. The following dialogue is an example of a technique used with an awesome young man named Mike. We use this critical technique to pull out a young person's dream—the starting place for all learning.

"Mike, if I came back to see you in ten years, and nothing could stop you ... You do know nothing can stop you, don't you? If I come back to see you in ten or twelve years and nothing can stop you, what will you be doing? Now remember, grades can't stop you. Money can't stop you. Your parents, teachers, and principals can't stop you. If nothing can stop you, what will you be doing?"

Mike smiles at me a little nervously. He's going to risk and tell me.

The audience knows what I am doing and so does Mike. Our previous work today developed trust between us. ▶

Mike finally looks at me and says, "I'm going to be a welder. A union welder."

I look at him and show how impressed I am. Then I explain what I am doing.

"Mike, I'm not taking your words literally. I'm trying to hear the metaphor of them. By doing that, I can see a larger picture. So what I'm hearing is, you want to create. You want to meld metal with fire. Goodness! Let's see, union must mean you want to be in an organization, or maybe be like your father, and then create big time with fire!"

As I speak, Mike begins to stand a little taller. He probably hesitated earlier because he wasn't going to say what most high school teachers and principals want to hear. He wasn't going to say he was going to college.

When we think of the pursuit of inner knowledge, we generally think of finite areas of study, usually connected with a degree or two from a university. To study almost anything today, you must follow a discipline. At the university level, you expect to see "-ology" at the end of every course description. To study rocks, you study geology; to study insects, you study entomology. These schools of thought are not interconnected. Each "-ology" represents a curriculum or a place on the assembly line of our paradigm. Yet these disciplines are quite new; they came to us

**education outside and education inside**

Now Mike looks at me with a proud set to his jaw and adds with confidence, "Underwater!"

"Whew," I exclaim. "So what you're telling me you'll be doing in ten years is you'll be a man, creating by melding metal with fire, and *nothing* will stop you!"

Mike is now standing ten feet tall. And I have Mike's dream!

The audience just saw how to pull out a youth's dream and look at it, without judgment, from a bigger place. As an educator, I have the information I need to create lessons for success for this young man. If I were his parent, I would understand where my child dreams of going. It doesn't matter if the life dream changes next week. I just got a glimpse of his core. I just tapped his desire—the place where all learning begins. ●

out of the scientific age. For thousands of years before that, the pursuit of inner knowledge was basic to being a human being. Cultures with full spiritual and emotional expression must find our isolated studies quite humorous, even peculiar. Therapy, for example, can be seen as a mind-paradigm response for a society that devalued heart and spirit and any comprehensive inner study. Our minds became confused by the repression of our souls, and our attempts to reconcile this were often superficial at best. As James Hillman says, "Why is there such a vast self-help industry in this country? Why do all these selves need help? They have been deprived of something by our psychological culture. They have been deprived of the sense that there is something else in life, some purpose that has come with them into the world."

What is more fundamental for understanding human behavior than the study of personality? Shouldn't we all be studying something so basic to our existence? Sandra introduced the Enneagram to the people working at our Center back in 1993. It gave us a box of tools that we could use for a lifetime of work. The Enneagram (thought to be over two thousand years old) approaches what might be called the nine challenges of what it means to be human. These challenges translate into personality "choices" that we all make. At first glance, you might think that the Enneagram is a psychological typology, similar to Meyers-Briggs. But on further look, you see that the Enneagram is much more fluid, which matches the concept of true learning. Whereas a typology states that a person is born with a certain personality and cannot change it (a concept that fits in the Knowledge Paradigm), the Enneagram posits that a person chooses his or her personality. Within each personality, specific choices of behavior can be made that move the person to integration or disintegration, to health or ill health. These choices give the person infinite potential for movement. Today anyone can use the Enneagram to identify the central motivations of their own character as well as the intentions of others. It can also serve as a nonjudgmental process that easily and smoothly takes the place of personnel evaluation. It helps people look at themselves and make their daily life choices more integrative and healthy; it excites people to better their performance. Using the Enneagram for personnel evaluation would displace the disintegrative judgment inherent in the current educational design. Such a change would have an astoundingly positive impact on our school system.

Helen Palmer describes the Enneagram as "one of the oldest models for understanding how people relate to each other and to the divine." Palmer also makes an interesting comparison of personality choices and paradigms of thought. She poses the idea that by choosing our personality we are actually choosing where we want to put our life attention. We enhance certain focal objects while eliminating others. This habitual way of filtering our attention creates a subjective reality or conditioned awareness that Palmer calls the "veil of illusion." This veil, or paradigm, alters our ability to be present to things as they occur.

Another interesting way to look inward is to study *projection* or *mirroring*. This concept provides valuable self-evaluation and helps develop responsibility along the way —something our society can dearly use.

Everything you think is a reaction or comparison to previous experiences stored within your memory. When you ascribe certain characteristics to others, whether good or bad, you are in fact expressing your own thoughts and values. This is called projection. Every thought is a personal interpretation of an event or action based on previous interpretations. The people and things that you "like" actually have values that you aspire to. The people and things that you criticize or see negatively represent what you wish to deny in yourself. No two people seeing the same event will file away exactly the same "truth" regarding what was seen. What would our world be like if we taught and developed this as a lesson of life for all of our children and teens? What would happen to racism or hatred? How would we then look at judgment, criticism, or humanity itself?

Opening up our children's education to the realm of inner study and connecting it to the greater world of outer study will alleviate much of the pressure of our current world. Where there is constriction and antagonism today, there can be freedom and unity. Where children have been trapped without hope, there can be infinite possibility for movement and even faith, which comes from looking at the bigger picture. Where there was little purpose to life, there can be all the potential that life has to offer.

# PART 2

# Wisdom Applied

# 6 Begin with the Child

*Your children are not your children.*
*They are the sons and daughters of Life's longing*
*for itself.*
*They come through you but not from you,*
*And though they are with you, yet they belong*
*not to you.*
*You may give them your love but not your thoughts.*
*For they have their own thoughts.*
*You may house their bodies but not their souls,*
*For their souls dwell in the house of tomorrow,*
*which you cannot visit even in your dreams,*
*You may strive to be like them, but seek not to*
*make them like you.*
*For life goes not backward nor tarries with*
*yesterday.*

—Kahlil Gibran, *The Prophet*

To make effective decisions about a child's education, we must begin with the child foremost in our thoughts. In our current educational system, which is based on the Bodymi or Knowledge Paradigm, true focus on the child rarely survives the journey through the maze of adult/ego needs. Our material consciousness leads us to begin with things, such as programs and curriculums, developed by people far removed from children. Educators are "mandated" to spend hundreds of hours responding to laws and policies developed by courts, legislatures, and decision-making boards—adults concerned with adult issues. The ever-present budget dictates educators' time and focus. Parents' needs, educators' needs, politicians' needs, and even commercial needs now take precedence over children's needs. Decisions are too often based on where openings exist in programs, which program budgets are already funded, or what we have done in the past. Such decision making is seriously ineffective. Knowing where openings exist in supportive programs may be important, but placements should never be made because of an opening. Money might be needed, but for true success it cannot be the single determinant or the beginning itself. Something that works well may be repeated over and over, but the reason for the repetition must be success for the child, not for security or tradition. What we are entrusted to do, by the children in our charge, is to think carefully of what children truly need and then act—putting in place a plan to attain the goal.

In this chapter we are going to look at specific strategies that work well with children. All of these strategies begin with the child. Many were put in place without special funding; some cost not one cent. Many had never been done before. All were successful.

## Responses from the Center

Angeles Arrien, author, educator, and anthropologist, was the first person I heard say, "The answer to any question you have or anything you need is around you at all times." I'm sure this is an ancient truth, but Angela's reminder is both poignant and appropriate at a time when we as a society have become removed from our own wisdom.

What Angeles often added is that finding answers is not so much a function of chasing after something new as it is removing the patterns, beliefs, and attachments that keep us from seeing. Teachers or parents looking for a solution to a particular problem with a child, or trying to understand a problem in their own lives, may find the answer right in front of them. One of the greatest ironies here is that just by holding this intention as truth, the solution begins to unveil. A person who becomes aware of a certain type of automobile for the first time all of a sudden sees dozens of them a day. They were there all the time; other things simply blocked the person's awareness. The opposite is also true. Don't believe there is a solution available to you and there won't be.

When Sandra created what she called the Children's Counseling Center, she began with the belief that the answers to the problems surrounding at-risk children *could* be found. She didn't doubt for a moment that the answers were close at hand. When I joined the Center a few years later and we began to seek solutions on a larger scale, we both embraced that inherent hope and faith as a foundation for the search.

Every step we took "began with the child" and created success for the child, or we tossed the step aside. We kept including different strategies and approaches as we awoke

Candy was a beautiful first-grader with long, curly, blonde hair who loved to wear fancy dresses and shoes that clicked when she walked. She had plenty of friends. She laughed and ran around the schoolyard, and in class she loved to hear stories about other children's lives.

As a newly appointed principal, new to the school and community, I was surprised when Candy's mother walked into my office to talk with me about the school's free and reduced-fee lunch program for children in need. A request for lunch was not unusual, but other things about this woman quickly got my attention. The school had two "feeder" neighborhoods, one described as "lower economic" that was located on the other side of town near the railroad tracks and factories and the other a well-to-do area in the hills. Parents from the hills neighborhood, like Candy's mother, normally didn't ask about help with lunch. What was even more unusual was the condition of Candy's mother. She smelled horribly. Her face and arms were severely bruised, and I saw needle tracks and sores on her arms and hands. I'd worked around drug abusers for years. I had no doubt about her addiction.

Candy was living alone with her mother. They were the talk of the neighborhood, not because Candy was so cute but because her mother was a known heroin addict and prostitute. No one could understand how Candy could be so "outwardly" well cared for.

School principals and educators are "mandated to report abuse." Believe it or not, having a heroin addict for a mother is not considered abuse. In this case, I could cite no measurable abuse, but that didn't alleviate my concern for Candy's welfare. Years of working with children and teens had taught me that mandated reporting sounds good, but oftentimes little is done by the agencies or workers you are mandated to report to. After the social workers or police representatives leave, the child is often in more danger, because now the parent has been alerted and will know to better hide the abuse. The word mandate has a powerful ring to it. The problem is, there is little dog behind the bark. Reacting to abuse instead of dealing deeply with underlying issues often makes the problem more systemic. By being forced to report abuse, many educators then stop there, feeling they have done their duty. Therefore no one actually deals with the depth of the problem. Needless to say, the abuse worsens.

I began checking sources to figure out my options for helping Candy and her mother. Were there any relatives around? What drug programs were available? How did they come to live in such an exclusive neighborhood? Where was Candy's father? I tried to circle the problem carefully. It had nothing to do with ▶

reading or writing or the other things I was supposed to be accountable for, but a child could soon be in danger and I couldn't turn away.

Apparently I was not quiet enough. The fourth week of school, Candy and her mother packed up in the middle of the month and moved—leaving no forwarding address. Neighbors saw them packing. I knew this was the flight of an addict, and the child would now be in real danger—a cute little girl on the streets was fodder for a hundred types of predators.

I called police agencies, but they couldn't help me, since no crime had been committed. I heard they moved into the mountains around Santa Cruz, where there were a lot of drugs. I called police and social services in Santa Cruz and the surrounding areas and passed on the task to people who I knew wouldn't deal with it as a number. Months went by, and years. I never found Candy or her mother—nor did anyone else that I know of.

In every public school, there are cumulative files kept under lock and key. Every child who enters school has a file with test data, immunization information, grades, suspension letters, and (what I like most) pictures of the child from kindergarten through fifth grade. Most people never see their files or even know they exist—but schools take these files seriously. Ideally, a file follows every child from elementary to middle to high school. If a child moves, the file is requested in writing and sent in the mail to the new school. Few schools, especially public schools, would accept a child without a file.

I think it would be safe to say that in every public school across this country, either in the front office or in the file room, there is an additional cumulative file drawer. It contains the files of children who have moved or not reregistered at the beginning of the next school year. The child, as far as the school is concerned, has disappeared. One middle school I worked at had hundreds of these files. Some were of children who probably entered private school. Some were of children who more than likely left the country. Many were variations on the story of Candy. ●

to the answers around us. To the one-on-one counseling design Sandra began with we added a mentoring program for children, so that they would have stable adults in their lives. Our society was massively creating crisis, so we set up a "No Holds Barred" program that unleashed a fury of energy when a child or teen was in danger. We began teacher training and parenting classes, the most successful of which was Sandra's Innerwork training for teachers, principals, and anyone working in the world of our children. This six-week training encouraged educators to be aware of their own personal "ego" work and to become aware of what they were bringing into the classroom or school. Innerwork became a very popular and effective way to create change in all of our district schools and beyond.

We added staff gradually, though our funding continued to be limited. Margene Janzen became our right arm as our administrative assistant, while Kate Nasse and Wendy Parker became the dynamic duo for counseling young children and families. A conflict resolution (Peacemaker) program, to teach children how to solve their arguments, was placed in the elementary schools under Marti Jacobs's leadership. Since our doors were always open to anyone who had a life/educational issue with a child, teen, or adult, we found ourselves in consultations throughout the day. We didn't advertise or seek money—a key to our design—and yet people began to flock to our Center as the result of word-of-mouth recommendations. This increased receptivity and broadening of focus moved us to change our name to the Children's Consulting Center.

In 1996, at the suggestion of superintendent Rick Damelio, we took on an additional task. We created a community day class for students who were expelled from the school district. The "community day school" designation is a legal one—part of our society's reactive response to the problems of children. Knowing that a legal response falls far short of a "child-based" response, I was not initially receptive to Rick's suggestion. After meeting with the teacher that the district had already chosen, Valerie Schwarz, I agreed to take on the task. Valerie and the aide we hired a few weeks later, Gene Dove, were delightful examples of what I learned to call master teachers. An opportunity was unveiling.

My reason for becoming the principal of this alternative class/school was different from what many people thought. I didn't want to create just another community day school responding to a legislated mandate. I wanted to use what we had learned at our Center to create an alternative community day school that would model to the school district and the surrounding cities what truly worked with *all* children—even the ones kicked out of the district. Our model was a combination of all of the "universals"—the things that work with anyone—that the at-risk children we had worked with taught us. We put all we had learned together into one neat package, what we came to call the Wisdom Paradigm.

## Consequences in Life School

Valerie and Gene got together and created the name Consequences in Life School—or CILS, as it was soon called. These two dedicated and delightfully crazy teachers were a dynamic duo. Their yin-and-yang approach to children was a slightly different version of what Sandra and I had found to be an unbeatable combination. Thus a key component for an effective classroom was put in place. All teens, especially ones in trouble, need good male and female role models.

The key task for Valerie, Gene, and me was to change the way education was defined and approached. Where change may be difficult in a regular school system, it was not so at CILS. These teens were often rude, uncooperative, angry, or depressed, and had current or past drug problems; all had been kicked out of at least one school, if not a district. They were so "challenging" that not a lot of people wanted to work with them. This was, in fact, part of the problem, which—since our method is to turn lemons into lemonade—we made part of the solution for these teens. To me, this meant no one would get in the way of what might work. As we had learned early in our struggles, change is difficult for many people. I used to joke with Gene and Valerie (and later with Kate and Greg) that they would have job security and free rein because no one wanted to deal with such severe problems. Legislation creating mandates for community day schools and other alternative programs is often motivated by fear. Although such motivation rarely helps find true solutions, it keeps away people who are scared and otherwise might interfere with new ideas.

One of our first moves was to get these teens out into nature and into life as much as possible. If you want to study the ocean, why use a book when the ocean is thirty minutes away? If some of the teens covet drugs, drive them to the Tenderloin district in San Francisco to see what drug addiction looks like ten years later. If you want to write poetry, where better to write than in a park or under a tree? And how about mathematics? Have you looked at the mathematical precision in nature, let alone in a city skyscape?

This move out of the classroom was at the suggestion of Rick Damelio. An extra Econoline van that the maintenance department had was sitting in the yard most of the year; the maintenance staff simply outfitted it with safe seating, and we put it to better use. It's a martial art strategy, to move with opposing energy instead of against it. Locking puberty in a classroom creates opposition and pressure. It contributes to what we call, out of frustration and paradigm nearsightedness, attention deficit disorder (which will be addressed in more depth later in this book).

Another important decision we made was also one of the most logical. Ask the question "Since teenagers are stuck on a fence between childhood and adulthood, how should we set up a structure *for them*?" The sensible answer is to put these "in-betweeners" with small children so they can "revisit" where they have come from, and with healthy adults so they can see where to go.

Most of the teens we were dealing with were forced to grow up much too quickly, experiencing life challenges that most of us face only in our nightmares. Giving them a little more childhood was positively nurturing. As for healthy adults, we have a huge resource that our society calls "old people." The teachers and counselors at our Center call them elders, which in itself is an important shift in thinking. (Chapter 10 goes into more detail about our work with elders.)

The teachers came up with the idea of letting the teens work with preschool children. Our preschoolers were physically, behaviorally, or learning disabled. In each case, both teenager and preschooler agreed to work together before a match was set up. The relationships that developed were truly inspirational. No matter what the teen had been through, the little kid would look up with admiration at this young adult. No matter what challenge the child was living with, the teen saw a miraculous and innocent child. The first thought that probably arose in each teen's mind was "And I thought I had it hard!" (The preschool teachers were also amazingly helpful in supporting these child/teen relationships. Teachers that work with disabled children, particularly young children, are often master educators, a concept discussed at length in Chapter 8.) The teenagers helped the little ones with their work and played with them in and out of the classroom. Adoration, not disability, was the focus of these relationships. The older students became heroes to the little ones, which was exactly what these teens—who had heard little but criticism and condemnation in their lives—needed.

Being with a child allowed the teen to be the learned one instead of the dummy. In some cases, if a teen had trouble reading, he or she was set up to help teach a first- or second-grade child to read. What does this reverse strategy do? You guessed it: the teen learned to read better. Of course, this worked with other academic challenges as well. The ages varied; the results didn't.

Another thing happened. These teens revisited their childhoods through the younger children. Having had most of their childhoods taken away by trauma, they were able to enjoy the innocence of being children—to play, fantasize, and learn again how to get along with others. The process was amazingly healing. Parents or other significant adults in the teens' lives who occasionally came to watch the young people at work were pleasantly shocked. Such visits would cause tears all around, healing the adults as well. They too had been traumatized by events leading up to their children's expulsions, and many of them also had lost their innocent years far too soon. In addition, the experience assuaged parental guilt and gave hope not only that their teenagers would be all right, but that they would be exceptional adults.

I'll never forget a huge young eighth-grader I'll call Sam, who came to our school after being expelled for extorting money from other students. He was also hanging around with some rough older teens and getting into occasional fights. He had been suspended repeatedly and his grades were failing. Sam was being intimidated at home but kept that fact buried. His relatives were raising him, and a couple of his older cousins were quite brutal and intimidating. Still, it didn't take him long to bloom at CILS, as did the vast majority of teens.

Sam learned at CILS that all of life is a lesson and everything—especially mistakes—can teach you something. Sam was always treated with respect by the adults at CILS and not judged for his errors. He learned to look at his life and to try to make sense of the world around him. The more sense he found, the more eager he became to learn. He learned that when you face your fear, your courage rises, and shedding guilt and pain makes you walk lighter.

He was reintroduced to the curriculums of his grade level after first reconnecting with his life, giving perspective and purpose to the learning. Instead of passing on anger, he learned to look at underlying issues, and to move with the same intensity in a positive direction. Instead of passing on fear and threats, he learned to give freely to others. Sam was soon known for his kindness and consideration to all, and he became a leader of the other teens in the room.

One day, out of Sam's sight, I watched Sam walk toward me. The hulking youth with sagging pants and stocking cap moved steadily and confidently down the center of the hallway, leading one child with one huge hand and another with the other. He strolled down the hall; he was their hero, their idol, their protector, their big brother. He moved with the natural ease of a parent. The contrast and the beauty—one monstrous in size, the other two so fragile and innocent—were amazing. He was walking these two miracles into life and getting on with his own, an elder in the making.

I learned early, after I let loose the current paradigm, that we must first tap into young people's dreams, then surround them with people who succeeded in those dreams—older people who are happy, well adjusted, and masters of their "trade." If a child wants to be a pilot, go with him or her to the airport. If a child wants to be an artist, get an artist to come to the child, or take the child to the artist. Look at the metaphor of a child's dream to get a better understanding of what the child wants; the metaphors underlying pilot and artist are much bigger than a job description. As a principal, I meet with parents and teachers to help them think of ways to nurture each child's dream. It matters little what the dream is, as long as it is healthy, and most life dreams and their metaphors are. Supply the child with books, educational software, and, even more important, mentors. Endless strategies can be pursued, modeling for the child how to *live* life.

## The Miracles Among Us

What is a miracle? Is it a vision of Mary appearing in Medjugorje, or rain arriving "out of nowhere" during a drought? Is it winning the lottery, or getting goose bumps while staring at the Grand Canyon? Maybe it is someone you love recovering from a serious illness. People have different views on miracles, but most would probably agree that they wouldn't pass one up if it happened to come their way.

Albert Einstein said, "There are only two ways you can live your life. One is as though everything is a miracle. The other is as if nothing is." Anyone who reads Einstein's later writings knows he belonged to the first group. Deepak Chopra has said, "If you really looked at a tree and truly saw what was before you, you'd fall on your knees speechless." It's not much of a stretch to say to a parent, "If you really looked at your child and truly saw what was there, you'd fall on your knees speechless." The same can be said of teachers and the children in their care.

It's safe to say that most people are not conscious of the miracles that are around them each day. Maybe being human means you have to walk in this world blind, and slowly reawaken. When was the last time you really looked at the sky, or the flower some might call a weed growing delicately out of an asphalt crack? Do you, like the rest of us, get distracted from what is truly important by the daily world with its irritations and diversions?

If you are a parent, do you remember your child's birth? Do you remember how your child appeared to you then? The miracle was as clear as day. And what about the first time you sent your children to school? Even though as an educator I had cared for hundreds of other people's children, my own were somehow different. It scared me sending something so precious off to someone I really didn't know.

The miracle of a child is very easy to see in a kindergartner: the innocence and joy, the wonder and excitement. Visiting a kindergarten class, you most likely grin and get goose bumps. Nearly everyone smiles and stares in speechless delight. Kindergartners are so perfect already. Why do we pursue perfection as adults when it was there all along? We allow kindergartners to be who they are, fully human. They play and dream, think and run, and we as adults don't judge them.

The premise here—a key point in this book—is that everything we as a society need to know about education and life is exemplified in the miracle that is the kindergartner. All of us still have that miraculous child, full of dreams, somewhere inside us. When we as parents or educators connect there, whether with our children or within ourselves, we move to a higher plane—the *bigger picture* of life.

People who work regularly with young children, particularly with kindergartners, will often say, "There is no such thing as a bad child." Yet we can lose that point of view quickly when we see the same child a mere six or seven years later. If you have gone to a middle or high school recently, especially if you are not an educator, the experience may have shocked you. The kids look tough, alienated, and different from the kids you probably remember. Some of this toughness may be a reflection of our times, but it is also just adolescence. The Bowery Boys or "pachucos" of the twenties, thirties, and forties certainly were intimidating.

But look at the kindergartner again, and then look closely at the teenager. Isn't what's in the little child still in the older child? Is it easier to see the similarity in your own child, or do day-to-day issues distract you? Can you remember your children when they were young? How about your childhood? Do you remember when you, too, had the whole world ahead of you?

When meeting with a group of parents or educators, I often start the presentation by handing each of them a small envelope. I tell them that the answer to any question they have about education, child rearing, or perhaps even their own life can be found in the envelopes. I then ask them not to open the envelopes yet.

We consider aspects of the child and the four realms as class goes on, diving deeply into issues of heart and life. At the end of an hour or so, I ask them to open their envelopes. Inside each is a picture of their child as a kindergartner, or, if that is not possible, a child from their school or community. The pictures rarely fail to bring gasps or tears, as the adults understand what I am proposing. The answer is in the awesomeness of the child. We all are walking miracles.

For graduation ceremonies for teenagers who come through CILS, I hunt all over to find a kindergarten picture of each of the graduates. Since so many of these young adults have disjointed lives, finding pictures of them is sometimes difficult. I enlarge and back what pictures I can find, and then I surprise everyone by bringing out the pictures at the beginning of the ceremony. Each youth comes up to the front of the room, holding up their picture. It makes for a tearful and beautiful contrast, particularly considering the life challenges these youth have mastered. It is obvious with every graduate that the innocent child is still in there.

At our Center, we try to see the kindergartner in each and every child or teen. We look beyond the tattoos and baggy pants, the pulled-down hat and sad or angry face. Parents and teachers learn to look in this manner, too. It isn't a false pursuit on our part, but a sincere appreciation. Isn't our task and responsibility as parents and educators to interact with all children in this place of delight and innocence? Such interaction is a critical component for success with people of any age. By beginning in this miraculous place, we go beyond ego and judgment, beyond the

*Every morning when I woke (when I was going to CILS) I was in a rush to get to school. The reason for the eagerness to get to school was because I knew when I got there, there would be someone who cared. At CILS the teachers don't pretend to care because they really do care. Whether you're in a good or bad mood there would be someone there for you 110 percent of the way.* —**J.**

surface. This facilitates an instant positive relationship. A positive relationship determines the success or failure of each interaction, whether it is part of an educational process or part of life itself.

Teenagers, particularly at-risk teens whose behaviors often echo the pain from their childhoods, respond exceptionally well to this approach. They have had enough parental and societal lies, hurt, and judgment. At our Center, we show them worth and respect by meeting them in this place of wonder and nonjudgment. The interaction that then takes place is different. Instead of feeling the judgment they have come to expect from adults in authority, teens sense acceptance. Children, too, are more perceptive than we give them credit for. Little children who sense unjudging adoration will squirm with delight. Children and teens trust adults more when they sense this spiritual connection. They feel "something bigger," and it feels good. Especially with teens, the communication that then occurs comes from an entirely different level than normal conversation. By remembering and contacting this "forever kindergartner," we can work in a realm of success and acceptance. Part of the solution for a healthy society can simply begin here.

It can't surprise you that Gandhi was right after all!

## Finding Sense Where Only Trouble Appears

*Everything a child does makes sense!* This premise is critical to the Wisdom Paradigm. We, as a staff at CCC, remind ourselves of this "truth" regularly. Parents and teachers visiting the Center are used to my pointing at a little paper with this statement pinned up next to my work area. Believing there is sense will motivate you to find it. Not believing there is an understandable sense ("She was born that way," "He's just like his father," "It's organic") freezes people in their limitations.

Anger makes sense. Even violence makes sense—to the person choosing the behavior. Anger can be a healthy, self-preserving defense. People may choose not to tell you why they are angry, but I guarantee their actions appear sensible to them. You may not like what they do. You may not agree with their logic, but it is there. Depression is something else you don't want for your child, but it, too, has a purpose. It could be an internal refuge from an unhealthy situation. Hyperactivity may be awful to deal with at home or in school. You may want to change the behavior, but that does not deny its sense, to the child. In fact, without seeing this sense, you will most likely not reach any acceptable conclusion or change.

*If you see the sense through the eyes of the child, you can devise or uncover a solution to the problem*. Take the severity of the upset, the depth of the emergency, the pain and stress, and use them as motivation to find a solution—a true solution that comes from seeing the bigger picture.

Instead of looking at the child as the cause of the problem, look for the sense in the totality of the child's life. Instead of looking at the child's body or mind as the culprit, seeking to prove illness or "disability," look at the whole child, inside and out. Instead of trying to cover over the issues and sedate the natural expression of the problem with "medicine," seek the more difficult and more complete approach, the kind of sense that says, "Oh, that is where this comes from! Oh, that is what is going through her mind and heart."

Drugs are often a short-term solution at best, masquerading as a magic bullet. This short-term approach is very dangerous in the long run. Your child, you, and the entire universe have order. Get together and seek the order. Believe me, this seeking gives the young person hope.

It is our responsibility to see the sense, without judging the child. You can judge the behavior all you want, but don't judge the child. If you do, he or she will shut out your words. Whether as teachers or as parents, we are the protectors and the guides.

This philosophy is a tool anyone can put into their "life" toolbox. Pass on this "sense" and this way of solving a problem to the child or teen, and you are passing on a solution that can be used over many generations.

The attitude described above—being together in the solution, seeing the cause as outside the child, seeing as "bad" the behavior but not the child—immediately takes the pressure off of the child. The young person, used to being ignored or judged, is relieved someone is listening and seeking an answer. Even before you have found a solution, the child no longer feels trapped. Hope is a delightful solution in and of itself.

## One Hundred Coins

*All of the children gather at his feet, innocence in their eyes. Your daughter or son is there, as are all the sons and daughters to be born that day. They look down at the earth with excitement, knowing their journey will soon begin.*

*They come from and are the Spirit. They are part of the Dream. Their hearts surge with love and compassion, as naturally as the wind caresses the sky.*

*But this day they will emerge again with a body and a mind, foreign to and yet intertwined with this larger world, a constriction of circumstance appropriate for the task at hand.*

*He looks about him with an all-knowing smile, pausing as he peers into the depth of each child's being. Each has chosen parents carefully and each has chosen a specific Task. It is clear for now, it must be forgotten, and it will be remembered again at the end. It has always been the Way.*

*His giant hand reaches out gently, and he gives each child one hundred coins. He reminds them to choose their investment well, keeping in mind the Task they have chosen. The children look at their packet of coins and then down again at the four realms of life where their investment is to be made. They are familiar with spirit and familiar with heart, but these two new human realms, body and mind, are puzzling. Yet they invest their coins where they must.*

*With great care, your child chooses where to place his or her coins—as you did when you were a child—knowing, of course, their placement can be changed at any time in accordance with the Task.*

Where did your child choose to invest his or her coins?

Write down the realms of body, mind, heart, and spirit, and then place a number beside each to show where you believe your child has invested, the total not to exceed one hundred. There are no right answers. The coins can help you see your child's uniqueness.

Doing this exercise with your spouse or other children may give you information on family dynamics and insight on how each of us sees differently. Since we each have a different task in life, isn't that difference not only appropriate but necessary?

Do this exercise yourself. Consider your own investment as a child. Then think about how your investment changed during different stages of your life, according to your needs. When you were a child, *body* may have been more important than when you were in college and your *mind* needed to take precedence. Maybe when you fell

*I'll admit that before I went to CILS I thought it was funny to yell and cuss at teachers, I also thought it was cool to get into fights. So when I got to CILS, I thought I'd try to be funny and yell at teachers. It didn't turn out the way I wanted it to (I used to love getting yelled at). They sat me down and made me talk out my problems.* —**S.**

madly in love or experienced a painful loss, *heart* became your needed consciousness.

Is your child experiencing difficulty in school? Look at his or her investment. Does it match the cognitive design of our educational system? Remember, the Knowledge Paradigm of our current system says that to be bright is to have a highly developed brain. How might a child who has chosen to invest a proportionately larger amount of coins in the heart or spirit realm do in this system? Or if your child has invested more than half of their coins in their body, how might sitting in a classroom challenge the investment? Also, scientists have found that using your brain actually stimulates the growth of brain connectors, just as using your muscles develops brawn. How could this finding affect a child or teen who in the past was convinced he or she was not very intelligent?

This exercise has helped hundreds of parents and teachers understand a little more clearly how our personalities sometimes don't match systems of learning, and how each of us is unique. You can be anything you want to be. Use your *heart* more, and compassion, empathy, and love will grow within you. Awaken to the *spirit* that is around and within you, and you will naturally become more spiritually conscious.

Some parents who do this exercise get frustrated when they see that their child is different and doesn't fit the school system. I always remind them that their child is *beautifully different* for a reason. I tell them, "You probably will not change your school or school system. Leave that to me. But what you can do is be aware of your child's life expressions and stimulate them outside of school." If parents particularly stimulate their child's realms of body, heart, and spirit *outside* of school, they will create a balance with the highly cognitive thrust of our current educational system. In other words, if children get to dream or write poetry a lot, or run and play outside of school, they won't be as frustrated when doing the more cognitive tasks in school.

Let's try another example. As a teacher, I often saw children or teens have temper tantrums over a simple name-calling incident or a bad grade on a spelling test. Obviously, any incident can be a "last straw," but what if this same child spent time truly pursuing life dreams inside or outside of school? Would missing a spelling word or being called a name have much consequence? Such incidents could then be seen from a different perspective. They might even be funny. It feels so exciting to pursue dreams, to freely express the heart, or to play to your body's satisfaction. Or maybe school isn't stimulating your child's mind enough. Let him or her really get exercise with projects of their own—but remember, this pursuit must be from the child's desire, not the adult's.

Bringing teachers into this way of thinking has a dramatic impact. Teachers enjoy this more open concept also because it frees them to begin their approach with each child a little differently. It allows them to develop projects specific to a child's interests and desire, and to remember that desire is the first step in learning. *No desire, no learning*. So if you as a teacher get good at hooking this desire, think how much more effective you will be. If you as a parent get good at hooking this desire, imagine the support you will provide for your child's life learning.

## What Is Your Strength?

Let's look again at the four realms of being—the body, mind, heart, and spirit quadrants. Have you invested a lot of coins in one area? Are you proud of your superior intelligence, or are you particularly sensitive to matters of the heart? Are you a natural-born athlete or a young devotionist? Well, I hate to say it, but in the words of Caroline Myss, author of *Anatomy of the Spirit*, "Whatever is your greatest strength is also your greatest liability."

Most people would say Albert Einstein was born a genius. Looking at intelligence in a different way, you might say he invested nearly all of his coins, at least for the majority of his life, in the mind realm. His obsession with the mind through his work in physics and mathematics took him away from the other realms. He ignored the emotional side of his life, spending nearly every waking moment with his theories and his work. This fixation on the cognitive world caused him to become alienated from his wives and children. In his later years, he made a major shift because of the great pain inflicted by this relationship challenge. By looking at and learning from the pain, he gained compassion and was able to add that to his cognitive strength. Heart and mind combine to create wisdom. After his death, Einstein was not only recognized by the physicists of the world as a genius; he was also adopted by the philosophers of the world as a sage.

As Einstein learned, our greatest strength—our "gift" —may also be our weakness. If you study the childhoods of geniuses, you'll see a pattern. The sensitive or introverted child goes to the mind as a refuge, a place of safety from what is perceived as the scary "outer" surroundings. No one can bother the child in the mind. He or she can hide there, in books and internal thought processes.

Einstein's gift kept him frozen in the mind. Maybe it felt so good inside and looked so scary outside that he shifted all of his coins to the mind. After developing his mind even further by focusing so intently on this one area, he earned worldwide acclaim. In fact, he earned the respect and awe of millions. When you are put on a pedestal and applauded for one trait, why change? It apparently took the divorce from one wife and the death of his other wife, the alienation of his children, and the horrors of World War II to propel Einstein to reinvest his coins.

In a society such as ours that is preoccupied with image and the body, what is one of the greatest "gifts" we all have been programmed to long for? Good looks, of course! Don't you wish you had a gorgeous face or a knockout figure? Well, if you were born "gifted" in the body realm, you would undoubtedly find that people stare at you and often comment on your beauty or on how lucky you are. Wouldn't you want to invest a lot of coins where it felt that good? But what about the flip side of the coin? Spending every waking hour in the body realm is not going to benefit your mind or your heart, let alone your spirit. Your gift could become a serious handicap.

Think of the athlete who is also gifted in the body realm. Do you usually think of an athlete as spiritual or intelligent? Rarely. Neither attribute is part of the standard image. If you can receive money, fame, and adoration for focusing on your athleticism, why do anything else? The gift keeps you there.

How about the stereotypical guru who sits in the lotus position staring upward into the sun, going blind physically because he's blind to the miracle of life and body he has been given? Or the cleric who spends so much time in prayer that he never understands the very earth he was born on?

Think of a poet who writes with compassion and deep feeling. Doesn't the intensity of emotion make the poet want to stay in the heart realm? Perhaps the poet fears that leaving it would mean losing that unique ability to be in touch with the senses.

To be whole, we must be balanced in body, mind, heart, and spirit. Shutting off any realm for great length of time will cause a crisis in the blocked area. Remember to think of the four realms on a continuous circle—spirit leads to heart, heart to mind, mind to body, body to spirit, and around again. We usually spend less time in the realms adjacent to our gift or strength. So your challenges are in the realms of life just before and after your gift. Is your gift in the body? Then your challenges and prime areas of work will be in mind and spirit. Are you exceptionally spiritual? Then your challenge will lie in the two nearest realms of heart and body, and so on. This design can help you pursue balance and fulfillment; it shows you where your work lies.

At first, it is important in life to follow your gift. When you emphasize what children do well, they develop esteem, confidence, and identity. But as we begin to grow, we need to move to other areas for balance, usually after we have risen to a level of success in our area of strength. We can then focus on another realm, and then another, continuing this movement to balance all our lives.

# 7 Let Us Truly Solve Our Problems

*"Don't accept that what's happening*
*Is just a case of others' suffering*
*Or you'll find that you're joining in*
*The turning away"*

—D. Gilmour and A. Moore, "On the Turning Away,"
© 1987 Pink Floyd Music Publishers, Inc.

Have you ever wondered why the biggest problems in our society never seem to go away? We have become so resigned to violence, drugs, racism, gangs, hunger, and homelessness that we consider them the norm. Think of familiar comments like "These horrors have always been around, and they always will be" and "Welcome to the real world."

Michelle Karns gives an interesting explanation of how this resignation comes about. She says that, first of all, we wait for a crisis to occur. When that crisis hits, we respond with a lot of energy. We feel good because we are responding, but since we are not looking for the cause of the problem, the problem is not solved. At best, that specific difficulty temporarily goes away. When the next crisis arrives, as it always does, we again gather our forces, expend a lot of energy, and then sit back again. This happens three or four or maybe a hundred times, until we are so exhausted that we give up and accept the problem. This way of reacting to problems rather than digging deeply for answers *before* problems arise is now part of our paradigmatic pattern.

As we have already discussed, our society's paradigm is a framework of thoughts and beliefs through which we see and approach the world. These basic beliefs underlie nearly everything we do. Some serve us well and some—as has come to light on our streets, and in our homes and schools of late—are a disaster no longer in the waiting.

One underlying belief of our society today is that there is a right way and a wrong way to do almost everything. And if I'm right (guess what?), you must be wrong. It is either one way or another, and since it doesn't feel good to be wrong, we all want to think we are right. Self-centeredness, waved like a flag as individual freedom, is also at the core of our societal paradigm. This accentuates further the need for "me" to be right.

Have you ever met people whose first reaction, no matter what the problem, is to point fingers at others? That doesn't bode well for those people's relationships, let alone long-term happiness, but many of us have been taught to react that way. This behavior is disastrous, because finger pointing alienates others and stops us from being introspective and learning our lessons. Hence the problems remain, and worsen.

Any time there is a crisis today, whether in a community or on the national scene, it does not take long before fingers are pointed. Whether it is a shooting, a budget crisis, or a simple mistake in judgment, the fingers quickly appear. Even with tragedies as heartwrenching as the shootings in Littleton, Colorado, it took very little time for the shock to wear off and for the lawyers and "adults" to start placing blame. This mentality keeps us from moving to true solutions because this "judgment" causes alienation. People become so irate or full of fear that they expend their energy dealing with the attack rather than dealing with the actual problem. A society that responds to problems rather than actively seeking preventive solutions will always have plenty of crises to react to.

Our penchant for using law and law enforcement to "solve" problems is another example of reactive behavior. You may already know that our prison system is one of the largest employers in the country. Last year my own state of California was ranked number one in prison spending and yet number forty-one in spending on education. The figures differ slightly depending on who is looking, but they are shocking however you compare the "investment."

I have heard it said that "we are a nation of laws." Laws assist societies that are too large for direct communication between members, as most are today. Yet if relied on too heavily, laws can take away communication as well as diminish the sense of community. Looked at from this angle, the quote is not encouraging. People who think in terms of "right and wrong" often believe "proper" behavior can simply be mandated. Laws become a reactionary response to problems rather than a contributor to true solutions. It is sort of like believing that the slogan "Say No to Drugs" will stop drug addiction. If it were that easy, would we have today's drug problem? Most cultures, including the Judeo-Christian one, have a commandment that says, "Thou shalt not kill." How is it working?

Eric Hoffer, writer, labor leader, and philosopher, eloquently stated the problem: "When mores are sufficient, laws are unnecessary. When mores are insufficient, laws are unenforceable." Mores come from the depth of our consciences. Laws are superficial at best. Societies, and educational systems, must seek the deep understanding that comes from the realms of heart and spirit. We must dive deeply into the ocean of life and stop being afraid of leaving the surface.

Our society today is enshrouded in law. Don't get me wrong. I am not arguing for a decrease in police support. What I am proposing is *more* support, but in a different way. At a conference on violence prevention a couple years ago, one of the lead speakers (a top law enforcement officer in California) shocked the audience and earned a round of applause when he said, "The deep problems of our society cannot be solved with more laws, more prisons, and more reliance on police personnel alone." The increasing violence—children killing children and mass murder after mass murder—speaks for itself. What we are doing isn't working. To solve societal problems, we need a deep, systemic, and *different* approach.

One clear problem-solving approach begins with a common, three-pronged design that our society hasn't implemented well. The design has three levels of action: *crisis intervention, intervention,* and *prevention.* It takes all three to stop a problem! In *crisis intervention,* we are responding to an emergency. Think of police or fire response, or medical emergencies and disaster response. Crisis intervention is absolutely necessary and everyone supports this work, especially when you are part of the emergency. We appreciate, for the most part, the heroes who respond for us. To do crisis work, we of course must have a crisis. Crisis work begins after the problem has reached dire proportions. It deals with the fire after it is flames. It is not designed to investigate where the fire came from or keep it from recurring. This is "level-one" work, just as the body is the level-one paradigm of the four realms of being (see Chapter 4).

Level two is called *intervention.* We toss the word around today as if it were synonymous with solution. It is not. Intervention is our society's more systemic approach to larger problems. Medical staff, social workers, counselors, and teachers work at this level. Here we feed the hungry; nurture the dying; counsel the unhappy, violent, or depressed. Intervention is difficult work that takes an enormous amount of energy and resources, especially if this is the bottom line of our problem-solving consciousness. Unfortunately, it is. We fool ourselves into thinking that giving solace to a starving person is a solution to the problem of hunger. It most certainly is an act of goodness;

any time we take such action, we are giving back to our community and to humanity. But intervention, just like crisis work, begins only after the problem has started. It does little to address the problem's true cause.

The third level, that of *prevention* (or, as I call it, the *true solution*), calls for deep thinking. Here we must plan and act before a problem even arrives, which takes forethought and a sense of responsibility beyond self. Prevention can be done by anyone or any society that has experience working at this level.

What if we were to nurture our children's inquisitiveness and give them opportunities to deal deeply with problems, their own and their society's? Practice in the heart and spirit realms prepares anyone to operate at the prevention level. Compassion takes depth. Understanding life dreams is about as big as it gets. By dealing with emotions, children and teens strengthen their heart realm. Exercise your arm muscles, and your arm gets bigger and stronger. Exercise your mind by thinking, and you become more intelligent. When you exercise your "heart," you become more compassionate and better able to deal with the emotional side of life. Exercise your spiritual nature—"play in the world of the bigger picture"—and you become stronger spiritually. Moving to the bigger picture, literally as well as metaphorically, gives you a bigger perspective. Removing attachments to ego allows you to look without judging and without personal bias. Not only can you see more options; because of your unattachment, you can act on them.

Societies that approach problems on the crisis level and with intervention strategies will fail in the long term if they do not move on to prevention. In fact, avoiding level three will cause even more of the same problems. Implementing only the first two levels ties up energy, resources, and time in the false idea that the problem will go away. It also creates a sense of relief that keeps people from going to the next, more important stage of prevention. Prevention strategies, on the other hand, actually relieve stress and provide more energy. When what you are doing truly has the desired effect, energy grows and is contagious.

The excitement of crisis intervention is addictive. It's a rush responding to a fire or meeting an important deadline at work. Because the work is difficult, it also makes us feel, after the crisis is over, that we have really done something. And we have! But the danger arrives when our sense of accomplishment makes us stop at this level.

Intervention work has a similar dark side. It is life consuming. People who do intervention work often spend their entire career giving. But after thirty years as a children's protective service worker, probation officer, or counselor, you may feel you have paid a heavy price because no one is stopping the flood of problems.

If Mahatma Gandhi were to look at how we try to solve problems, I bet he would recommend that we shift our way of thinking (that paradigm shift we've been talking about). He'd undoubtedly suggest that people interested in crisis intervention work in prevention instead. Don't waste time and energy trying to convince a drug dealer that drugs are bad. Forget about telling the American tobacco industry that cigarettes damage your health. And you won't convince the war department that peace is better. People who are attached to what *is* don't believe that change is needed. We can change the consciousness of the entire country by focusing on children. Remember what Gandhi said.

A simple problem-solving technique I learned from Sandra is very effective on a day-to-day basis. Any time you really want to look for the cause of a problem (which is, of course, basic to finding a solution), you ask yourself "Three Levels of Why." For example, suppose a child is cutting school. You talk to the child, the parent, and the teacher and come up with your first possible why. Maybe *he doesn't want to go to class.* Instead of stopping there and simply disciplining the child, as is very common today, you ask yourself again, "Why?" Why doesn't he want to be there? Maybe this time he says *he doesn't feel good there.* Well, let's go to the next level of "why." "Why doesn't he feel good there?" Because *he has other things on his mind and the teacher gets frustrated at his inattention and yells at him.*

Now we are getting somewhere.

Now you ask, "What do you have on your mind?"

*"I heard my parents arguing and my father said he was thinking of leaving home."*

Finally, a level of solution. The steps you take now, knowing this information, are definitely different from the steps you would have taken after step one. By the way, it often takes four or five steps (not just three) to reach the true cause.

Keep some things in mind when approaching Three Levels of Why. Always remember a child should never be expected to answer questions. Your prior work on your relationship with the child should have set up trust and a foundation for communicating, and the child's readiness will determine the technique's success. I believe that all children want to be happy and healthy, and I treat them that way every day. If they know I am coming from a place of compassion, and I regard their welfare as paramount, they will talk to me. If they think I have another agenda or issues of my own, they will freeze up and not talk. If you have done your work, the child will consider you safe enough (wise enough?) to open up to.

Questioning begins with a child's desire for help. For the most part, if children trust you, they will talk. Remember, readiness is critical for all deep work. You wish them well, offer to be there when and if they want to talk, and *back away*. They will return when they are ready. Obviously, if a child is in danger, the expediency changes things. I then tell the child how important I think he or she is. "And when I feel you are in danger, I'm going to do something to help or protect you. Can you help me help you?" Keep in mind that everyone wants to be loved and to feel safe. If you offer love and security, without attaching to them any other issues, the child will respond.

Teenagers are back-away artists. They back away by saying "I don't know" or "Who cares." They do this more often than children do because they have had more negative experiences with adults who have other agendas. Respect their distance and they will come back to you before you know it. Teenagers are (beautifully) like wild animals. Show them you want to touch them and they move away. Show nonchalance, but no threat, and they come to you.

The Three Levels of Why technique works well on you, too. Sandra used it with the staff at the Center to uncover core issues. Sometimes we bury our true issues under superficial ones. The next time you are in a bad mood and want to trace it back, try Three Levels of Why. I think you'll be pleased with the results. Get a trusted friend to try the technique with you, or your spouse or teenager. It may take practice. Model Three Levels of Why for your child.

We can stop drug use, violence, hunger, and every other ill on the planet today. That is not what you have come to believe, is it? Well, it is true. People who are comfortable looking deeply at issues of life can create solutions. Operate in the realms of heart and spirit with the intention of solving these seemingly endless problems, and you will be astounded at how simple the answers are—simple to see, but not necessarily easy to do. Working in the world of prevention/solution is lonely, yet very rewarding. But that loneliness is going to be a thing of the past, starting with the next generation. Or maybe starting with you.

## The Importance of Fear, Pain, and Stress

*This being human is a guesthouse.*
*Every morning a new arrival.*

*A joy, a depression, a meanness,*
*some momentary awareness comes*
*as an unexpected visitor.*

*Welcome and entertain them all!*
*Even if they're a crowd of sorrows,*
*who violently sweep your house*
*empty of its furniture,*
*still, treat each guest honorably.*
*He may be clearing you out*
*for some new delight.*

*The dark thought, the shame, the malice,*
*meet them at the door laughing,*
*and invite them in.*

*Be grateful for whoever comes,*
*because each has been sent*
*as a guide from beyond.*
—Rumi

In our society, we are taught to avoid pain, stress, anger, fear, and depression. We associate these maladies with illness, unhappiness, and, in the extreme, death. We even have drugs, doctors, and therapists to help us with our avoidance.

What if this is backward? What if the avoidance actually causes more stress, fear, and pain? What if it sidetracks people, or even an entire society, into debilitation or ill health? What if this one belief is key to our society's unhealthy circumstances?

I am not suggesting here that pain is something to seek. We do not wish suffering on anyone. But life has a way of bringing challenges, and, as with everything else around us, there must be a reason, even for pain.

Angeles Arrien points out that many cultures for thousands of years have believed that "any fear you face no longer exists." And as Sandra has reminded me repeatedly, "If something has been around for a couple thousand years, you might want to pay attention."

Stop and think for a moment. What is pain for? Pain is a warning, something to make you stop doing a particular behavior that might hurt you. Pain makes you look at that behavior and learn not to do it again. Stress is the same thing, expressed differently. Depression, too, makes sense. Depression seems to be a natural response for an introverted person feeling trapped, just as anger is a natural expression of an extroverted person feeling trapped. Why do these "negative" emotions exist if not to show us where we are trapped and to prod us to take healthy action? When we ignore these "flags," the problems continue and in fact worsen. By taking action with good intention toward a solution, we obtain relief as well as knowledge. Even if our attempt is not fully on target, we still feel relieved because we are no longer hopelessly stuck.

All of the teens who come to our Center have been suspended from school because of misbehavior; some have been to juvenile hall. Many have been expelled from the

When a teenager is sent to our Center, I usually shock them a little with my approach.

"David, I hope that whatever behavior got you sent here comes back."

David is silent. He looks at me like I'm crazy. He has been sent to us because he yells at teachers and refuses to do what they ask of him. He has over fifteen days of suspension this year alone. From looking at his discipline file, it appears he has had problems with anger since age ten. He is now fourteen years old.

"Is anger what got you kicked out of school?"

He nods.

"I believe everything has a reason, David. Anger has a reason. Depression has a reason. Everything has a reason." I pause and let the words sit there for a while. Since David doesn't know me, he sits quietly, not fully trusting me.

school district, two cities wide. Their expulsion hearing was undoubtedly filled with warnings of "If you do that again, you will be . . ." Troubled teens have heard dozens of adults command them to be good. Adults threaten that if the problematic behavior returns, they will do something severe as punishment, but little time is spent searching for answers.

I say let the behavior return. It is not that I am a masochist. I don't like negative feelings. I just know we need to

"To me, anger is trapped passion. I'd like to help you untrap it. Don't get me wrong. I don't want to make you angry. I just want to have the opportunity to help you understand and give you other options so you can get on with your life." I look at him for a moment. He's looking at my blind dog, Madison. Madison stares at him with love in his smoky eyes. I know he sees better than I can.

"We have seven months to do this. Let's get it done before you go on to high school."

David again looks at me funny. I don't believe he understands how this is going to happen, but he looks like he's hopeful, and that is exactly the place we will begin.

"Do you hear the passion in my voice?" He nods. "That's anger with a positive direction." I smile and, finally, so does he. ●

look at depression, fear, and anger, or nothing is going to change. Such an opportunity to study the true issues may not come again. The next time they get in trouble, the teens may be in another school or another city, more than likely where no one will help them find the life lesson that lies underneath their problems.

To solve problems we need to open doors, not shut them. When I work with teenagers, I tantalize them with a different way of thinking. I know that just by taking their fear, pain, stress, and depression seriously, with the *intent* of understanding, I give them some relief. They've seen alcohol and drug abuse, lost dreams, unhappy or abusive marriages, and dead-end jobs—some of the ways adults model to children how *not* to deal with life. And all of these "life troubles" are more than likely never discussed, let alone understood.

I have learned to look at school cumulative files carefully. I don't begin by looking at test scores; I look at teacher comments, letters, notes of custody battles, or family name changes. I look for the sense or order that might precede certain behaviors. Dramatic events or changes in teens' lives—in anyone's life—can cause pain and anger that may last for years. Part of my work is to uncork that anger and give it direction. The crucial thing is to talk with teens in a way that doesn't judge and that separates their behavior from them as people. The most important thing I can do by talking in this fashion is to pull out some hope. Treat them with respect, and indicate that together you will go deep to find answers, once and for all.

Remembering that *the answers we need are always around us,* I pay attention to what my tai chi teacher, C. K. Jeung, taught me—move with the energy, especially in times of apparent threat. "Don't fight what comes at you. Look with 'soft eyes' and you'll see everything around you. Seek to move with the energy coming at you, in balance, seeking understanding."

What if fear is the predecessor of courage? Hasn't everyone courageous started with fear? Don't fight the fear; step into the fear and turn it into courage.

What if anger is undirected passion? Let's take anger, give it purpose and direction, and turn it into leadership.

What if depression is the by-product of stymied emotional expression? Give depression "expression" and turn it into art, dance, and music.

What if hyperactivity is undirected energy? Show the child or teenager how to move into action using the energy in a way that has purpose to him or her.

Adults are astounded when they see children and teens learning such skills and acquiring such power. What originally was seen as a problem becomes a sensible step in the recipe for life.

To demonstrate to parents and teens the importance of dealing with pain, I use a comparison of Mahatma Gandhi and a derelict in the gutter. For me, the difference between them is primarily one simple belief.

Let's compare Mahatma Gandhi with a man sitting on a street corner in Big City U.S.A. seeking coins to buy a bottle of wine. Believe it or not, both are miraculous human beings. At the age of kindergartners, they were both innocent and playful and had their whole lives ahead of them. What produced such different lives?

Let's look again at the two different attitudes toward pain. Whereas the person needing wine was taught to run from possible pain or fear, Gandhi was taught not to run from fear but to try to understand it. The man living on the street thinks that avoiding pain (especially the pain of failed expectation) works, because he's been doing it for years now and he's still free (and on the run). Gandhi knew that avoiding pain only worsens the problem you are avoiding. Whereas the one man turns his head, so as to avoid the unpleasantness, and goes to the park to drink, the other knew that if a person withstands pain—even the pain of being beaten—he will become stronger than he was before. Whereas the man on the street fears going to a hospital or getting arrested, Gandhi dared the British to send him to jail. Every time he was incarcerated, he was given more time to plan and think; he became stronger both spiritually and politically. To a large degree, Gandhi forfeited his physical health to show the Indian people that sacrifice from one person can benefit the many. Undoubtedly there are more differences between these two men—differences of character, if not karma—but my point stands just the same. A single, yet critical, attitude toward life can turn a life from one of grandeur to one of pathos. One of the powers and responsibilities of being human is that we can choose.

Each of us chooses beliefs that we hold dear. We hold them so dear that, in some cases, we would die rather than change them. This sounds dramatic, but it is true. It is true of the addict, who will more than likely die because of something related to his addiction, and it was true of Gandhi, who died for his beliefs. We all die, but it's the way in which we *choose* to die that is significant.

Some of our beliefs may be defense mechanisms that we adopted as children. For example, what if a child learns that the immediate world is not a particularly safe place? Parents may ignore the huge, potentially painful issues of life—what counselors and psychologists call the "elephant in the living room." This expression is used most often to describe a house where one of the parents is an alcoholic, but our households today have many more types of "elephants." Addictive behavior and its destructive results are obvious, yet there is an unwritten rule against discussing them. A child in a house that has hidden fear and anger sometimes learns to tread lightly to get by. Dodge artfully, or the adult(s) may descend upon you out of fear of being forced to look. At least this is the perception of the child or teen, and the perception alone can create the same fear and avoidance.

Say a child's parents are unhappy. The mother is stressed by a crisis in her life, or the father is convinced there is too much ugliness in the world today. "No one needs to focus on the *bad* stuff. Let's look on the good side." The child learns quickly, for whatever reason, that parents (and other significant adults) don't want to talk about, let alone deal with, the unpleasant things in life. Maybe drink is their refuge, or work; maybe telling jokes keeps things light. So the child picks up certain behaviors for self-protection and dealing with life. Being funny works. Having a quick mind that can divert people or conversations away from what might be unpleasant is very helpful.

This thought pattern sets the stage for such children to avoid unpleasantness or pain. They pursue fun, are generally happy-go-lucky, and move around a lot in the classroom. As adults they move from house to house, job to job, and relationship to relationship. They may like sports or jobs where they do lots of different things, changing their focus often. They probably like cars, preferably fast ones, and don't stay in one place long, in thought or in body. This personality is called the "forever child" in many books on personality.

It's hard to stay in the "fun" realm and avoid so much other life for any length of time. Some people with this "forever child" personality develop healthy addictions, like exercise routines or playing sports. Some, despite their penchant for diversion, take life challenges head-on and become mature, wise, and awesome. An unusually large number, however, seek to stay in this "fun" place. Parties are a prime method, but it's hard to party day and night, though many try. It's just a matter of time before they'll need a little help staying light. Television works well, as do video games. Drugs and drinking are prime methods, but the irony hits full force here. People can't stay "up" forever; in fact, drugs cause the opposite reaction. When people come down, they respond by going up again, even higher and faster. The fall then becomes farther and harder. The expression "You can never get enough of what you don't need" powerfully describes this frenzy.

Laws of the universe cannot be beaten. (They were made by the same mysterious force that made us.) Whatever goes up must come down, not sometimes but always. People who choose the "forever child" personality with its need to seek heights will also have canyons of depression in direct correlation to the height of the flight. When significantly out of balance, this personality type takes on the characteristics of what has been labeled the manic-depressive.

Our society reinforces this "forever child" tendency by promoting superficial thinking on television, in books and movies, in sports and everyday conversation. We are taught to seek fun and games, to be "cool" and not to bring people down. We clothe our outer selves—with face-lifts, breast enhancements, and hair implants—and ignore our inner selves.

No wonder the "forever child" personality is common in our country today. Though it is sometimes labeled a disorder, it is not a *dis*order. It is in order, because it makes perfect sense. We may not like the sense, since it can have unhealthy expression, but it is part of the recipe our society hands out. We operate entirely on the surface of the ocean, with our metaphorical ski boats and bathing suits. We don't deal well with depth in any form. We have made the avoidance of pain and fear into a multi-billion-dollar industry. Because we avoid fear, we pass it on. And what you bury, you also carry.

By understanding how children learn to run from fear, we can design and pass on strategies that can then move them to health. A child who wants to run from fear can easily be shown at home or in school how good and safe standing still can feel. We all know that a teacher or parent can teach a child tools that can be carried for a lifetime. First, the adult holds the child's hand, literally and figuratively, and walks him or her safely into that fear. One key point to teach is that scary situations, when faced, are nearly always less scary than we have imagined. Making a child feel secure is one way of stopping the need to run. Perseverance, the virtue underlying this security, is worth its weight in gold; it is the balance point for a child who wants to run. I define perseverance with children or teens as "holding fast three steps past where everyone else wants to quit." This teaches them not simply to stand, but to stand long enough to outlast others and become courageous. Adults cannot let their own issues mask, block, or deny a child's fear. Instead, we need to show the child how to face and understand the fear.

Reducing the number of surprises or unexpected movements and having routines help create calm. So does talking gently. Establishing a nurturing, loving, and protective structure around children is key to a teacher's (or parent's) success. Simple rules, with no inordinate flexing of those rules, help children feel safer and misbehave less. Now implement those axioms systematically in the classroom for young children and see what happens.

The simple strategies presented in this chapter have an astounding effect on children, families, and communities. Applying these techniques in all public schools (within the structure and philosophy of the Wisdom Paradigm) will not only reduce drug addiction but also stop the proliferation of gangs. We haven't mentioned gang participation, but take my word for it—gangs are a substitute for family and security. They are not groups of angry, sociopathic teens, as they may seem. Gangs are composed of scared, paranoid teens trying to look tough and belong to a group so they feel secure. Strategies that create a sense of belonging, surround children in security, and focus on life stop drug addiction and the need for gang protection. The Wisdom Paradigm frees children from the fear of a false societal and educational design. We will explore specific wisdom techniques in Chapter 11. By refocusing on people instead of things, by seeing education as coming out of the child instead of from the adult, by beginning with the welfare of the child instead of from adult needs, we create what is needed for health. Drug addiction and gangs exist only in societies that fail to do these things.

Most parents who attend one of our trainings or come to the Center for a consultation have children in trouble. It pains them to see how death, divorce, judgment, and other hard things affect such innocent beings. I tell parents that we will have to go deep into the pain, all the way down, to view the larger picture needed to find true solutions. But I also ask them to trust that I won't leave them there.

After we have reached the bottom and all of us have no doubt cried, I use a technique like the following one to bring them back up. They usually cry again, but this time they are crying out of hope instead of despair.

Think of someone in your life, or a person you have read about, who is extraordinary. Others guide their lives by this awesome person's example. It can be someone from history or someone from your family. He or she can even be a character from a novel, a story, or a comic book.

Have you thought of someone? If not, keep thinking.

Write down the person's name on a piece of paper. This is just for you. No one else will see it.

Are you finished?

If I am in an auditorium with a hundred people doing this exercise, I then begin pacing the aisles and challenging the whole group. "I'll bet you one thing. Regardless of whom you picked, I'll bet they all have at least one thing in common.

"I'll bet that all of you thought of someone who had great pain or immense challenge in his or her life. I'll bet that person didn't have all the things our society currently promotes as measures of success—a two-parent home, a nice house, a new car, good grades, a high-status job.

"I don't care if you thought of your mother or Mother Teresa, Maya Angelou or Superman. I'll bet whoever you picked became great *because* of the trials this person had, not in spite of them.

"Am I right? The degree to which you dive is the degree to which you can rise. No diving, no rising."

Now let's look at your child's life in this light. Does it look any different? What previously looked like a life heading for the bottom looks quite different, doesn't it?

And what do you suppose the life of the extraordinary person you thought of looked like when he or she was young?

## The Language of Metaphor

When we think of metaphor, we undoubtedly think of poetry. We use metaphor to contrast characteristics or essences of things and people. Metaphor helps us move to a larger, less finite way of thinking so we can, for example, compare the beauty of a rose to the miracle of a growing child. But metaphor is much more powerful than that. Metaphor is the language of the Wisdom Paradigm. Deepak Chopra, esteemed endocrinologist and philosopher, considers metaphor so important that he calls it "the language of the Universe."

Metaphor is an excellent example how two plus two can sometimes be much more than four, which is another way of saying that "the whole is greater than the sum of its parts." Arthur Zajonc uses the bicycle to illustrate this synergism. Take a bicycle apart, lay the parts out on the ground, and you have a collection of tires, chains, bolts, and metal bars. If you haven't seen a bicycle before, you would never believe what it could do when assembled. Though you have all of the parts in front of you, separately they do not contain the potential of their combined whole.

Just as with the bicycle and its pieces, metaphors are far bigger than the words that express them. Whereas the Knowledge Paradigm focuses on singular "facts," the Wisdom Paradigm plays with the essence, so as not to become frozen in only one aspect. Metaphor expresses fluid meaning. By staying unattached through movement, metaphor opens more possibilities to exploration. The immense world of mystery (the realms of the psyche, emotions, and spirituality), because it is not literal or linear, can best be tapped with a tool that is also not finite.

Currently, in the Knowledge Paradigm we are taught

to seek *the* answer, *the* best things, *the* reality. A number of problems arise with this way of thinking. First, reality changes. Second, by believing that everything has one right answer, you automatically make all other answers "wrong." "If I am right, then you must be wrong." Thus begins the world of conflict and judgment, the mind-set that is the foundation of fighting in our personal lives and our society. This singular belief in rightness has caused wars for thousands of years.

With metaphor, you can explore the larger *essence* of something. By thinking in metaphor and moving to the essence of something, you de-emphasize the attachment of your ego and therefore diminish the points of collision with someone else's ego.

Let's look at some specific examples of how to use metaphor while exploring the problems of our children and teens.

Parents, teachers, and principals deal with a number of misbehaviors on a regular basis. One is stealing. As a school principal, I used to think I dealt with children who steal in a fairly effective way. I would listen to the child's version of what happened first. I would have a discussion with the child on the power of honesty, and give an appropriate discipline for the offense. Undoubtedly we would get to "You probably wouldn't want someone stealing from you, would you?" This question would lead into a talk about trust. That doesn't sound bad, does it? The frustration came when the child went out, a day or two later, and stole again. I often took this repeat offense personally because I believed we had established a relationship (that's ego on my part!). Well, there is a better way.

First of all, you may be astonished that children rarely, if ever, need what they steal. Even when children steal money, they invariably blow it on silly things or give it away. In either case, the money is gone before any consequence can be made of it. Obviously, children are not stealing for material reasons, though that is what we always assume, coming from a material paradigm (based on the body realm). So moving beyond that, to the realms of heart and spirit, what is the metaphor of a child who steals? To use metaphorical thinking, it is helpful to think in questions instead of statements. What if the child is stealing to replace something he or she feels is missing? What if that "thing" is not material and more than likely is something the child isn't fully aware of, something of an emotional or spiritual nature? Remember, spirit is beyond words.

So here we are with a child who perceives something missing that is, to that child, rightfully deserved. This "rightfully deserving" part is the permission for the theft. The child feels stealing is permissible because he or she deserves whatever the object is.

Remember that everything makes sense, and our task is to see the sense through the eyes of the child. Invariably, when I meet with a child who steals repeatedly, something important is missing from his or her life, a father or mother, or, more simply, attention from a parent. Many times the child perceives that others receive more caring or nurturing. How do you find these things out? You have a trusting conversation about *life* with the child. If you come from a place of love for the child and show an attitude of nonjudgment (basic *universals* discussed at length in Chapter 8), this conversation will be easy. You then use your gut/intuition to take steps toward a potential solution. The child can't always express "why," but if you follow your intuition, then plan a strategy to meet the missing need, you can see if the stealing will stop.

For example, if you think the child is missing attention from a parent, bring the parent into the process as part of the solution. Give an appropriate discipline, because discipline does make the child feel more secure. But deal with the stealing as separate from the child's self-worth. Talk to the child about the inappropriateness of the behavior. Deal with the behavior as being inappropriate, not the child. Then move beyond the discipline to nonjudgmental strategies to stop the stealing. Together with the parent(s), and maybe the teacher, plan and implement strategies for positive attention. Our school system is geared to find out what a child *doesn't* know or do well. We want to find out and nurture the opposite, what he or she *does* better than anyone else. Better yet, find out what the child perceives is missing and talk about it honestly without judgment. Talking alone usually lessens the misbehavior. Step back and see what happens. Does the stealing stop? If not, plan and implement another strategy. Keep going until you hit the jackpot, following your intuition and discussing strategies with other concerned adults along the way. The odds of finding a solution are very high.

What if a child repeatedly lies? Lying is untruth, so let's

look at truth from a larger perspective. Maybe the child perceives that some basic truth or secret is being withheld from him or her. It might amaze you how often this is the case. One of the most common secrets involves a missing parent. Dad is gone, but no one says why. Or the child's mother is in jail, but no one wants to damage the child by talking about it. This "hole" of truth or information will be filled in by the child's greatest fears. Though withholding information may be well intended, it actually creates a festering sore that gets expressed by misbehavior such as lying. This scenario is not uncommon. Remember, in our society today, we have a strong aversion to dealing with unpleasantness.

Think of a child who often gets into fights. Your first and foremost responsibility is for the safety and security of those involved. Mete out consequences for the inappropriate *behavior*, not for the bad child. The child is always good and loved; it is the behavior that needs adjustment. But instead of only dealing with the obvious aspects of fighting, take time to ask, what might be frustrating in this child's life that would cause him or her to lash out in this manner? Keep in mind that the bigger the "lash out," the more important the issue is to the child. Does the child feel someone is hurting her or him? Pain doesn't have to be physical. Does the child feel threatened, or somehow trapped in violence? Does the child feel unheard? Has the child asked for help in other ways, but the pleas went unanswered? Gather information, involve those needed to create safety and understanding, and then take action.

Two more examples of common behavior beckon to be

understood through metaphor. I believe that most behavioral problems encountered with small children are related to the child's perception of the loss of love (mother archetype) or the loss of security (father archetype). Whether the loss is real is almost insignificant. By assuming it is real, you can look, in an unattached way, to see if the behavior you are worried about has parental issues at its root. Children who are "phobic" at the beginning of a school year will more than likely respond to strategies that make them feel more secure in life. Children looking for attention who are sad or seeking friends too vigorously may need love. Plan some strategies that give comfort, warmth, and caring attention to the child, and see how he or she responds. A simple touch on the head or a personal greeting in the morning can do wonders. Make the child feel special, not just another student in a seat. You'll be amazed at how often you will hit on a solution.

Together you are seeking an answer—not you alone as parent, teacher, or principal. I do this strategizing side by side, as an equal, with the parent and/or teacher. Skills or tools you learn to benefit one child can then be shared with other children down the line.

## Integration vs. Disintegration

> *We can easily forgive a child who is afraid of the dark; the real tragedy is the man who is afraid of the light.*
> —Plato

Imagine that you are standing on the railroad track of life. There are only two ways that you can go. One direction takes you closer to your life's goal, your integration, while the other leads you away into disintegration. Integration beckons you from your core. Disintegration tempts you from the surface.

When you integrate your life, the parts of who you are become more connected inside and outside of you. Given your circumstances in life, given your family line, given your task, one direction will be best for you and everyone else involved. Given those same factors, the other direction—disintegration—will cause your life to become disconnected. Move in the direction of integration, and your life will come together with more strength, understanding, and wisdom. Move in the other direction, and the ground will be set for ill health, stress, and unhappiness. You have been given the choice—a prime characteristic of being human—to make decisions that promote growth or deterioration. Integration's extreme might be called wholeness, enlightenment, or holiness, while the disintegrative extreme is neurosis or evil. People become saint-like when they systematically move beyond their own needs and dedicate themselves to the needs of all. Disintegration occurs when people refuse to look at their life issues and systematically feed off others to justify the backward movement. As complex as life can be, it is also supremely simple in its order.

Our children and our teens find themselves in troubled situations because the value system our society promotes is clearly disintegrative. We are being tempted to do what is blatantly unhealthy for everyone.

What if you could head off negative behavior in your own life? All change begins within you. Before you can begin to work to better society at large, you must work on yourself first. Let's look at a simple way of doing just that.

Keep in mind a concept that Carolyn Myss clearly states: "It doesn't matter what decisions you make, but it matters absolutely the intention with which you make them." You can't go wrong if your intention is truly a good one for all. Intention should be your decision-making guide; good intention moves you toward integration.

Certain "flags" help guide the way, and certain concepts underlie each choice. When faced with a problem, step back and look at what is before you. The "right" decision, the one that is good for all, usually stares you in the face. The tough choice is most often the right choice. The easiest, fastest, or most tempting decision is usually the wrong decision.

The chart below lists some integrative and disintegrative factors. (Can you think of any more?) When these traits are clearly evident, pay attention and choose your direction on the track accordingly.

| *Flags of Disintegration* | | *Flags of Integration* |
|---|---|---|
| easy | — | takes determination |
| fun | — | awe-inspiring |
| quick | — | long enough |
| short-term | — | long-term |
| good for *you* | — | good for *all* |
| shallow | — | deep |
| false | — | true |
| tempting | — | intuitively attractive |
| artificial | — | natural |

| | | |
|---|---|---|
| holds fear | — | transcends fear |
| holds anger | — | transcends anger |
| manipulates others | — | truly helps others |
| hidden | — | open |
| judgmental | — | nonjudgmental |

Did you note that the items in the left-hand column are concepts that society often tells you to pursue? The "Hollywood" ideal put forth in commercials, television sitcoms, magazines, and newspapers (to name but a few sources) is a recipe for disaster. Not just for some, but for all. Not just for now, but from ancient time to future time, from Liverpool to Timbuktu.

Imagine further that the railroad tracks you are standing on are on a mountain. The tracks going uphill certainly look more difficult than the tracks going down. Your life task—metaphorically, of course—is to climb the mountain. While easy is tempting, something basic inside of us knows we must go up the mountain. We must toil to get where we truly need to go.

Keep in mind that we are talking about life decisions. At no time am I professing that people should not have fun or do what is easy on occasion. However, at times that affect your life, pay attention to the flags. Making a decision about what you are going to do for a few hours on Friday night differs significantly from where to go to school or whether to risk your life. A concerted effort to pay attention to these flags will have a dramatic impact on your relationships, your family, and even your community. You know, the little things.

# 8 The Master Teacher

*In the beginner's mind there are many possibilities, but in the expert's mind there are few.*
—Shunryu Suzuki

To understand what makes the learning process work most efficiently, we only need to look at the master teachers who are all around us. If our current educational design is in fact limited, we might want to pay attention to someone who finds extraordinary success despite this limitation.

I bet you have met a teacher who seemed to be able to teach anyone anything. Odds are a person comes to mind quickly: someone you had as a teacher, or someone you met at one of your child's schools. Such teachers are the ones you never forget. If we look carefully, I think we might find at least one of these marvels in every school. All of the kids know who they are, and so do the parents. They seem to approach teaching a little differently from most. What if these teachers have similar traits or approaches? What if we could identify what these *universal* qualities are? Well, guess what—we can!

Think of a teacher you had whom you'll never forget. Something special went on between the two of you that made the class memorable and the learning more profound. Maybe your third-grade teacher opened a world for you. Maybe a middle school teacher turned your life around, or a high school teacher or college professor moved you to pursue a lifelong vocation. Take out a piece of paper and write down the name of the teacher who comes to mind.

Now ask yourself, "What made it work? Why did I learn so much from this teacher? Why is he or she so memorable?" Take your time and write down the qualities that made it happen.

When I do this exercise with a group, I compile the participants' lists on a board that everyone can see. Depending on the size of the group, the list usually contains fifteen to twenty different things. Then participants vote for the traits they consider most significant, generally trimming the list to five or six things. We can say that these items are potentially *universal* to the art/science of teaching.

Hundreds of teachers and parents have done this exercise. What astounds every group is that after they go through the process of identifying master teaching traits, I pass out a list of *universals* that I have already typed up, and the lists match. The qualities really are universal; they may be worded differently, but their essence is the same.

By identifying what works for all children, and all people, we can improve our educational approach. The educators at the Center—after years of working with children, teachers, and parents—have produced a list of universals.

In doing so, we do not seek set answers; we leave the door open for further discussion and consideration. Yet the following teaching traits have been found to work with *all* children and transcend *all* curriculum areas. A successful educator (what I call a master teacher)

- Loves children
- Seeks to see or interact with children without judgment
- Knows how to establish and maintain a "key relationship" with a child
- Makes children feel special
- Is excited about life
- Makes children feel secure
- Is creative and playful
- Loves learning
- Is organized for the child
- Seeks to know him- or herself

The last trait, "seeks to know him- or herself," is not readily identified by teachers and parents as a universal. Sandra Larragoiti, my wise and learned colleague, added this trait because she considered it critical. I include it here because I, too, believe it is key to successful teaching.

What is peculiar about these traits? First, I would say that most, if not all, are obvious. To someone who has taught for decades, they are no-brainers. What most surprises me is that none of the universals are cognitive-based traits. They all have to do with emotional bonds, issues of worth or acceptance. Stop and think about that. We have an educational system built on the concept that learning is done through the brain, and yet the determinants we found that make education work have little to do with the brain! In fact, I think it would also be safe to say that the majority of these traits are not taught in teacher preparation courses at all. Perhaps including them could be one of our first steps in shifting our educational paradigm.

Now let's look more specifically at these universal traits. The first three are the foundation blocks; the others are significant supporters.

### Loves Children

I did say that these are obvious, didn't I? Love really is the key. Without compassion, understanding, adoration, and appreciation of children, everything else is off target.

People in schools who love children—principals, teachers, custodians, or secretaries—stand out. They smile in pleasure at children's innocence; they play in the schoolyard when they could be doing something more "serious." They don't enjoy sitting in the teachers' office complaining about children. Their rooms are charged with delight and joy. Concentrating on the love children show so easily allows us adults to refocus on what is important, and forget about day-to-day distractions or larger diversions like politics or money. The middle or high school educator with the ability to see the kindergartner still inside the teenager has a distinct advantage. Connecting with this innocent child within probably can't be done without love. And doesn't everyone want love? Love is encompassing and contagious. It spreads to the children and teens, to coworkers and parents. It is very obvious when it is there and just as obvious when it is not. Decisions made from love begin with the welfare of the "other," not the "self."

For a brief moment, let's look at the opposite side of this coin. Many people don't want to talk about this side, but I would be remiss and my conscience would bother me if I didn't lay it on the table. During the time it has taken me to write and rewrite this section, three sets of teachers have asked me if I was going to put anything in this book about people in schools who hate children. They begged me to do this. So with the intention of helping us all understand, and plan alternative strategies so we can get on with our work in a healthier manner, let's look at a "Universal of *Un*successful Teaching": people in schools who hate children.

A couple years ago, I spent some time with an associate superintendent of schools (from a different school district) who was dying of cancer. Facing death has a way of clarifying issues. He and I got into a deep conversation about life and, of course, children. We were talking about the revolutionary changes needed in education when all of a sudden he paused and became quite serious. He said that if he could do anything to create positive changes in education, he would get the "child haters" out of our schools. I was surprised by his comment but knew all too well what he was talking about. When I think back on my own schooling and my decades as an educator, I can remember dozens of master teachers who helped make children's lives better. But I can remember as well a few rotten apples in the barrel. I have also had the unpleasant experience of watching unhealthy teachers, principals, custodians, and even PTA officers and school board members feed off children in a hurtful and systematic way. I like to think such misdeeds are rarer in education than in other fields, but education deals with something so important—what could be more important than helping to form children's lives?—that the risk of damage is magnified.

Where do these nightmares come from? They come from an unhealthy society that doesn't emphasize looking at life. They come for the money or the calendar, but not for the love of children.

We've all seen educators who are angry at the world, or who had horrible childhood experiences. One of these unhealthy people can scar thousands of children, so their effect is not something to downplay or ignore. How do we get these people out of education? We get them out, ironically, in the same way you get a child or teen back on track.

Our current evaluation system is judgmental and confrontational. I propose just the opposite. Move with the energy, like in martial arts. We get child haters out of education by emphasizing the universals of successful teaching, especially when hiring the next generation of teachers. We *love* them out. Creating an effective system of education that models and stresses love will solve the little and big issues in one fell swoop.

I have successfully counseled teachers and principals to move to life pursuits they truly loved. Some educators stayed in teaching with a renewed joy, having touched on some unprocessed life issue that had been holding them down. Some left education to be healthy and happy—as Joseph Campbell would say, to "follow their bliss."

Let's get back to the importance of love for successful teaching. Our current paradigm, the Knowledge Paradigm, has helped us develop our minds to an impressive point. Researchers of the brain tell us that by using the mind, we build the mind's capacity. As the body builder builds muscle tissue, the brain builds dendrites. Taking this "truth," let's now use our hearts and spirit to build the capacity for compassion and understanding of humanity. Since such action is wise, we call this the Wisdom Paradigm. Instead of discussing brain research, we can talk about heart desire. Instead of focusing on cognitive development, we can emphasize compassion and love. What would happen if we just talked on a regular basis about the power of loving children? What if in elementary and middle school we systematically and authentically poured love on our children? Might the next generation be more compassionate? What if in teacher preparation programs this prime factor, love of children, was put forth as an absolute for success, both for the children and for the teacher? We would raise the next generation of educators in a way that would have a revolutionary impact—a generation raised on love, wisdom, self-reflection, and education that comes from life lessons.

## Seeks to See or Interact with Children Without Judgment

> *When error no longer creates the dismal weight of failure, new opportunities open for discovery. A mistake is not an occasion for self-reproach or guilt, but a method to find new ideas and facts. For in all of the Ways we make mistakes, and as long as we do not recognize them and do not learn what they will teach us, we are imprisoned by them. When instead we take full advantage of them, we are less afraid of erring and readier to risk.*
>
> —Piero Ferrucci

The second universal is one of the most important. I have yet to work with a group of teachers or parents who did not list this trait as a component of what made their own education work. Such unanimity gets my attention.

Ironically, one of the great challenges of being human is that we must toil to reach a level of understanding that takes us beyond the "right and wrong" duality of things. To be human is to judge. But to be wise, healthy, happy, and fulfilled humans, we must learn not to judge. We may never complete this lesson, unless we attain the level of Christ or Buddha. However, it is clear that we are supposed to try.

When anyone at our Center works with educators, the importance of being nonjudgmental is underlined, posted in neon, and repeated over and over. *The degree to which teachers will be successful with their students is in direct proportion to the degree to which they are nonjudgmental.* It is that critical. Assessment is important. Measuring progress is essential. But if assessment is done in a manner that has even a hint of judgment, *you* as a teacher will fail. Judgment stops the educational process. *To judge is to reject.* If the child senses personal judgment rather than a judgment of his or her actions, the learning process—if not the relationship itself—will be damaged. As soon as someone senses judgment, a wall goes up in self-defense. The creative, positive energy needed to pursue learning is halted.

Think of your own experience. Have you ever had a job evaluation by a supervisor? How did it feel? Even when the supervisor is commenting on how wonderful you are, you are still apprehensive. As a school site administrator, I was required to spend hundreds of hours a year in a process designed to evaluate the performance of my teachers, aides, and clerical and custodial staff. I learned quickly that every hour I spent judging, I destroyed the hours I spent building relationship, another base component of success in education. The judging felt good.

As principals, my colleagues and I used to complain to one another on a regular basis that when evaluating someone we could say ten supportive or complimentary things, but as soon as we said something that was regarded as critical, the person would become rigid and oppositional. All the person would remember of the conference was the one point perceived as critical. At the least, the teacher or staff member would go away less energized. Somehow that seemed contradictory to my job. And don't forget what I said about the time involved in this process—time away from other tasks, masked in a way that is supposed to make everyone more efficient. The need to evaluate was handed to us as being right and responsible. The irony is, it is just the opposite. Sacred and learned texts in nearly all cultures warn that *when you judge, you will be judged*. Judging is a never-ending negative pursuit that is one of the temptations of the human condition. When we perceive education or teaching as a job, we invite this limiting judgment. When we see teaching as a life pursuit, self-evaluation is joyous and purposeful work, part of what you are here to do. Learn to look at your own efficiency and effectiveness, seeking advice and observation from nonjudgmental peers who understand the bigger picture beyond ego. Learn that what doesn't work well is often more important than what goes smoothly the first time. What appears to be strength is often something that freezes you in place and stifles creativity. Self-evaluation is very different. It actually increases motivation.

There is a reason for judgment in our society today, and this reason is also at the heart of much of the violence we see around us. When—as in our current societal paradigm, the *bodymi*—the world is perceived as black and white, right or wrong, and, of course, good and bad, confrontation becomes the norm. To be healthy, all of us are supposed to see past this superficial dichotomy. As educators or as observers of education, we pretend that judgment of students in school doesn't cause damage, but our children and teens know better. As Friedrich Froebel, the creator of what we now call "kindergarten," warned, "For the children will teach us, and they will not be satisfied with half-truths." As challenging as it may be to implement nonjudgment in our educational system, there must be a way to do it, or nonjudgment wouldn't be one of the universals of successful teaching. Who was the teacher you remembered best? The one who was nonjudgmental. If the exercise were done in reverse, the exact opposite answer would come up, just like the proof of a mathematical equation. Who was the most unpleasant teacher you ever had? The one who judged you most. By moving your consciousness out of today's limited paradigm, you leave the realm of judgment. Listening with your *heart*, or standing back and looking at the world around you from the *bigger picture,* you are no longer bound by the ego constraints that create judgment.

Children immersed in the beauty and excitement of a learning process will instantly stop when they perceive they are being judged. You can see their shoulders sag, their eyes lose their sparkle, and their attention move away. Soon they put up an attitude of defensiveness to block what the teacher will say next. When students shut down in this manner, the process of learning ceases, whether the teacher goes on or not. Some students may complete the lesson, but they will retain nothing except

*CILS, you may think, is a school for troublemakers but in my opinion, I think of CILS as help for inside problems. My experience at CILS will never leave me. At a regular school, a teacher will give you work and expect you to do a good job on it. The thing they don't understand at regular schools is that not all kids learn at the same pace or even finish their work at the same pace. At CILS they give you work at your level, and there is no pressure into finishing your work at a certain time. You are able to do your work at your own pace, and you are also able to get all the help you need.* —**D.**

the pain (residue) of the judgment. Grading shuts off education faster than almost anything else, and changing the grading symbols only changes the form, which the judgment hides under. The color red speaks for itself.

If you talk to teenagers who have stopped doing anything in school or read accounts of teens who murder their classmates, you notice that there is often a clear expression of their having been judged by parents, teachers, or peers, usually all three. Alienated youth, feeling trapped by this alienation, will become violent with themselves or with others. This depressive or aggressive behavior is a universal animal response, from the harmless mouse to the dangerous tiger.

In my thirty years in the field of education, I don't believe a year has gone by when someone didn't want to revisit how the grading process is done or look at the great debate of promotion versus retention. And the amount of time and energy parents, teachers, and administrators spend talking about the negativity inherent in the multi-grade-level class is also shocking. I was on a grade evaluation committee my first year as a teacher, and numerous times hence; I chaired a grade evaluation committee prior to my stepping out of the regular role of school principal. The negativity, the alienating process, and the system's way of keeping the judgment process intact helped motivate me to do something dramatically different.

As I write this, the *San Francisco Chronicle* headlines a hot (and judgmental) educational issue: social promotions in a large local school district. The flak, of course, has become political and spread to the county and state levels. The irony is, both sides of the issue are missing the critical component of the problem—the design itself has created the "failure." The foundational concept that a "right" exists, and therefore all else is "wrong," creates this constant battle. Until the paradigm shifts, the problem will not merely continue but intensify. I have found from decades of personal experience running schools that when a single teacher, the principal, or the school's teaching staff as a whole simply *attempts* to reduce judgment, the strengthening in the child/adult relationships is astounding. Misbehavior can be dealt with in a quicker and more complete way because of the increased level of trust and the removal of ego-based issues such as fear or worth. As a result, all involved save huge amounts of time because the "lessons" are received faster and the recidivism is markedly reduced. Experienced deans, principals, and teachers will quickly acknowledge the importance of relationship work as a preventive to misbehavior. Removing judgment also creates another delightful side effect. People who favor judgment often feel they are motivating students by giving them a "kick in the pants." The opposite is actually true. Test scores rise when judgment is taken away.

Evaluations are a constant source of complaints and negativity. No one has found a way to make evaluation a smooth, healthful process, because something alienating cannot be smooth and healthful. Our current societal paradigm, and hence our educational system, is founded on there being a right and wrong, with the emphasis on wrong. From grading to grade levels to the philosophy of education itself, we are "efficiently" judging our way away from our true goals. The problem can be solved only by stepping out of the current mind-set and redoing the foundation itself.

Of course, judgment of the child exists in all sorts of fields—counseling, psychology, psychiatry, medicine, and the judicial system. In encounters with any of these professionals, as with educators, as soon as the child perceives judgment, successful interaction stops. This is one of the main reasons that many counselors and specialists in the psychological field are unsuccessful. Parents complain to me on a regular basis about the years of counseling, tutoring, or therapy and how much the child or teen hated going, and how little was accomplished. This lack of progress is a by-product of judgment. A professional can get the trust, the "ear," the mind, or the heart of a child only with nonjudgment. Take away the judgment and watch what happens. Children and teens love coming to the counselors at our Center. They actually come on their own, outside of regularly scheduled visits, to say hello or "just drop by." They ask to come to the Center even on weekends and holidays. Why? One important reason is that we don't judge them.

Even in special education, looking for "disability" instead of ability has the same component of judgment. In the least cases, it leaves the residue of judgment. In the greater cases, special education labels children "emotionally disturbed," and less than normal by birth. Though I chaired hundreds of special education meetings with wonderful, caring people, this inherited design never set well with me. The clinical design used by many professionals who work with children—and which is taught by most of our teacher preparation colleges, counseling departments, and medical schools—is built on judgment. We look for disease, for what is wrong, instead of focusing on what promotes health.

In our society, we get judged all the time. Think about your day today. Have you been judged yet? Judgment comes in so many forms—a spouse's suggestion, a commuter's horn, or a coworker's inadvertent comment. How does it feel? Can you hear a buzz or feel pressure in your head when someone is judging you? If you really want to understand how basic judgment is to our mind-set, try to go through a day without judging anyone. It is nearly impossible! But it is an excellent practice. The next time you are in a group of people, and you sense a subtle feeling of judgment coming your way, concentrate on how it makes your stomach feel. This practice is part of a Buddhist technique called "seeking soft belly" that is used to promote health. Judgment creates tight little knots in your stomach, your back, and even your face. This negative-energy expenditure is subtle and, therefore, often hidden, which makes it more debilitating in the long run. I wonder how many people's stomach or back problems come from years of being judged. The tension of being judged adds up. In its extreme, over years, it may be at the core of why some people snap.

We can assess without judgment. That sounds contradictory because our paradigmatic filter inhibits us from seeing this different way. Judgment stops movement, while nonjudgment allows for a continuous flow of positive energy. Best yet, nonjudgment feels good, and who wants to stop what feels good?

There are no mistakes, only lessons. Rather than beating ourselves up over a disaster, we can study it to see what information we can gain. Moving to the bigger picture, stepping back and looking at the problem as a life lesson, puts a person on the way to true learning, health, and happiness. Timothy Gallway's poem eloquently makes that point.

THE ROSE

*When we plant a rose seed in the earth, we notice that it is small, but we do not criticize it as rootless and stemless.*
*We treat it as a seed, giving it the water and nourishment required of a seed.*
*When it first shoots up out of the earth, we don't criticize the buds for not being open when they appear.*
*We stand in wonder at the process taking place, and give the plant the care it needs at each stage of its development.*
*The rose is a rose from the time it is a seed to the time it dies.*
*Within it at all times, it is constantly in the process of change, yet at each stage, at each moment, it is perfectly all right as it is.*

—Timothy Gallway, *The Inner Game of Tennis*

Here are a few ideas on the contrast between judgment and nonjudgment:

By judging, we illuminate failure.
*Instead, focus on success.*
Judgment emphasizes outcome.

*Instead, focus on the joy of the pursuit.*
Judgment stops interaction, attaches guilt like an anvil around your neck.
*Nonjudgment frees you of energy-depriving guilt and makes life feel lighter.*
Judgment stops listening.
*Nonjudgment excites the learner to hear more.*
Judgment stops learning (it fills the "forgotten warehouse" I discussed in Chapter 2).
*Nonjudgment frees us to retain more (it fills the box of the remembered).*
Judgment freezes action and limits experience.
*Nonjudgment encourages movement and increases experience.*
Judgment stifles faith and trust, and creates fear and doubt.
*Nonjudgment builds courage as well as trust and faith.*

Nonjudgment is a secret potion for success with children and life in general. Practice it and nurture it. Your life and the lives of the people around you will grow in joy as a result.

Let's look more closely at how to be nonjudgmental while working with a child or family. The most important step is listening to the parent or child tell their story, without judgment. I have learned to listen with the intention of simply hearing, not judging. I focus on the miraculousness of the kindergartner inside the child or teen. This approach is the opposite of the learned adult talking to the needy child. These people are not here just to learn from me; I am here to learn from them as well.

We then begin a discussion in which I ask clarifying questions, as an interested observer who delights in learning about another human being. Together we explore the issues involved, not from a personal standpoint, but from a bigger perspective. We might explore metaphors of the child's behaviors or discuss what might happen to anyone in these circumstances. By remaining nonjudgmental, I gain the trust and involvement of the person in order to explore possible solutions. We plan steps to take, and get excited about the possibility of their completion. This planning gives the person hope regardless of the outcome.

After we implement steps for the solution to the problem, we get together again to learn from each other what happened. With this information, we can plan the next move. At no time do we declare the rightness or wrongness of the initial plan. If it went completely awry, we can still laugh about it and gather information with the intention of moving forward again. This process continues until we hit "pay dirt," an approach with obvious positive results.

When we seek "the" answer, as in our society's current design, we are intimidated if it doesn't come right away. We make a move, stop, evaluate, and then decide whether we are right or wrong. If we're right, we get a pat on the back and move on to the next stop. If we're wrong, we have to decide whether to go on at all. This stop-and-go, energy-giving-and-then-depleting design doesn't work well. Taking one step forward and ten back isn't productive.

The nonjudgmental process described actually teaches children and parents how to solve problems on their own, without any "professional" or expert needed. Now that is a solution.

### Knows How to Establish and Maintain a "Key Relationship" with a Child

A "key relationship" entails combining universals one and two: it focuses on the child with love, compassion, and an appreciation of the miracle that is the child, and it is based on nonjudgment. This relationship creates motivation and desire in the student, and desire is the initial step of learning. If there is no desire, there is no learning. If a teacher sees him- or herself as the learned one and the child as an empty receptacle for this knowledge, there is little chance for learning to take place. In fact, it is even doubtful that the teacher will learn anything this way. I am reminded of the anonymous quotation "You will never learn anything by talking."

Piero Ferrucci, esteemed psychologist and philosopher, comments on the power of relationship: "At the end of the course, one can measure how much a student has learned about a given subject. But at a deeper level, the teaching of the subject was really only the pretext for a beautiful event shared by two or more people. The number of topics for study is immense. But the greatest masters of all teach the same thing."

### Makes Children Feel Special

If you feel someone thinks you are special, won't you do more, listen more, try harder, and more than likely perform better for that person? Again, this is common sense. This universal seems to be a combination of "Loves children," "Is excited about life," and "Seeks to know him- or herself." Teachers who love what they do will communicate this "special" feeling, but they first must be freed from "self" issues to be able to focus on the worth of "others." A teacher who was judged as a child and now points that judgmental finger as a form of motivation will motivate no one.

### Is Excited About Life

Excitement is contagious. No wonder it's an important factor in the success of a teacher. In fact, if you think about the people who attract you, one quality they more than likely possess to some degree is an excitement about life. It actually makes them physically attractive, whether they have society's traditional traits of beauty or not.

Excitement about life connects us back to the kindergartner inside all of us, before we took on fear and judgment. As children, weren't we in wonder of the miraculous and astounding things that surrounded us? For the most part, this eagerness is a normal state. We had to collect a lot of garbage along the road of life to lose it. Have you ever had teachers who lacked excitement and seemed always deeply burdened by life? How much did you learn with them? Odds are long that these people are highly successful teachers. Or if you are a teacher, have you ever had a time when you were troubled and lacked this excitement? (Haven't we all felt this way at some point in our lives?) How would you measure your teaching success at that time?

Education is the pursuit of life, an excited pursuit of the miracle that we are and the miracle that surrounds us.

### Makes Children Feel Secure

Two things are basic to a child. They long to be loved unconditionally, and they want to feel safe. Other than the primal need to stay alive, nothing is more basic to any human being than security and love. If either or both of these needs are not met, the child will seek them and not be attentive to lesser needs such as academics. Any child with security issues is not going to attend fully to class work. Any teacher who does not address this need through attention, structure, and sincere caring for others will wonder why some children stray in their attention or don't develop the trust needed to establish a key relationship.

### Is Creative and Playful

I doubt that anyone who has a sour disposition or difficulty laughing can be very effective with children or teens. People who laugh easily, especially at themselves, model how to stay unattached to ego. Remember the saying "If you can't laugh at yourself, your ego is attached"? Humor is a natural way to get beyond the right and wrong of things. It is a ground for the practice of nonjudgment (the second universal).

We need creativity to "play" with concepts of daily life, to move away from the standard way of thinking. Creativity and learning naturally go together, as do creativity and playfulness. By being creative and playful, we explore options, views, and angles others might not discover.

We all laugh freely and are creative as children. But in adolescence, we temporarily lose our ability to laugh and play—not by giving away the ability, but by letting someone else's fear or judgment obscure it. Remembering when we were children, going back in our memories, can help us laugh and create again.

In cross-cultural mythology, the figure of the Fool is often at the heart of change or truth. The way in which Fools "play" with issues frees them from the prison of righteousness or finite thinking. As a universal archetype, the Fool sees the absurdity within particular paradigms and loves to expose the hidden assumptions. All children have a little of the Fool in them, and teenagers especially delight in rediscovering it.

Denise Breton and Christopher Largent note in *The Paradigm Conspiracy*, "Fools are paradigm-savvy, since juxtaposing different paradigm perspectives is how Fools both amuse and enlighten. The Fool makes us question our assumptions, even everyday ones." These attributes are critical for successful teaching.

### Loves Learning

Just as teachers must love children in order to be master educators, they must also love learning itself. No one can be great at what they do unless they truly love it. Just as learning itself begins with the desire inside each of us, so does the "calling" to work with learners. Being a teacher has more to do with the heart than with the brain.

In the Knowledge Paradigm—the paradigm we are leaving—factual knowledge is thought to be the determinant of a good teacher. As we move from lower education to higher education, we expect the teacher to "know" more. College professors are, of course, at the top of the heap, as are specialists in medicine or jurists in law. But as anyone who has been a teacher or a student knows, having knowledge and teaching that knowledge are two different things. Haven't all of us had professors who are famous in their field but couldn't transfer that knowledge to a single student? On the other hand, we believe that "a good teacher can teach anything."

The emerging paradigm is one of wisdom acquisition, where some mysterious aspect of heart and spirit blends with the mind. Love, desire, life, and knowledge make for a richer educational soup than the mind alone does.

## Is Organized for the Child

A teacher needs to be organized. That is not much of a surprise. This universal comes closest to fitting our current educational design. But the difference here is *around whom the organization is based*. This organization is not for the teacher or to fit into a grade-level curriculum. This organization is based on the child's needs, the child's dreams, and the child's desired pursuits. If the other universals—love for the child, nonjudgment, the "key relationship," and humor and creativity—are in place, then this universal of organization will fall in line perfectly.

## Seeks to Know Him- or Herself

Being human means to have an ego with its issues of self, security, and power. Our prejudices, our basic beliefs, and our unfinished childhood issues affect all that we do.

In the first universal, "Loves children," we briefly discussed the importance of having healthy, self-reflective adults surrounding children. Just as a master teacher can positively impact thousands of children or teens over a lifetime, an unhealthy teacher can affect the same number in a negative way. It is critical that adults be aware of any unprocessed issues in their own lives that they might carry into the classroom. This awareness can be developed through many avenues or practices.

The practice of dealing with unresolved issues is paramount. Not only does it help us understand our own motivations, but it also helps uncover and understand the unfinished work from our own childhoods. Understanding unfinished issues is a key to happiness. Remember the universals "Is excited by life" and "Loves learning"? These two regions are positively influenced by nonjudgmental self-reflection. A practice of self-reflection also allows us to stop relying on one of the most detrimental processes in education today, personnel evaluation. Evaluation can cause alienation, antagonistic labor relations, and even lawsuits. Whereas evaluation damages relationship, self-reflection strengthens it. When evaluation seeks to measure performance, it actually stymies growth. A self-reflective process is so effective and satisfying it beckons the person forward.

One effective practice of self-reflection is the nonjudgmental process Sandra Larragoiti set up. Innerwork helps teachers begin or continue a daily practice in resolving life issues. Teachers, superintendents, custodians, and school secretaries alike find this process invigorating and effective.

Parker Palmer, educator and author, has also pursued this important field of self-reflective practice, working with the support of the Fetzer Institute. Parker begins with the premise that "good teaching cannot be reduced to technique; good teaching comes from the identity and integrity of the teacher." From this foundation comes a focus on teacher character formation as one of the critical components of teaching.

Our children are worth whatever it takes to find true masters to fill our classrooms. When our educational system begins to lead the nation—rather than simply replenishing the assembly lines—a whole bank of mature, wise, and selfless people will begin to enter our teacher preparation programs. At the same time, our universities are being challenged to actually prepare teachers for teaching. Until now, they have been teaching students how to use a boat to climb the education mountain. The universals highlighted in this chapter are proven forms of mountaineering equipment.

# 9 Attention Deficit Disorder: Downside Up

*Where the speechless unite*
*In a silent accord*

—D. Gilmour and A. Moore, "On the Turning Away,"
© 1987 Pink Floyd Music Publishers, Inc.

The national organization for Children and Adults with Attention Deficit Disorder estimates that over six million children, teens, and adults are currently diagnosed as having a form of attention deficit disorder (A.D.D.). Many of these people have had antidepressant or stimulant drugs prescribed for at least part of their treatment. A recent report published in the *Journal of the American Medical Association* states that two-to-four-year-olds are now being medicated with Prozac and Ritalin. According to this limited study, the use of such drugs has increased nearly 300 percent in the past year. My own experience working with families bears this out. The newest drug combination I see being prescribed for grade schoolers is a mixture of Dexedrine and Prozac. These powerful and controversial drugs scare me. I find it alarming that they are being prescribed to small children. Medicating is a good example of how—though we may mean well—we are teaching children to bury life issues, to do what is easy and look for simple "pill" answers. This surface mind-set fosters drug abuse, pure and simple.

As previously discussed in this book, when a problem grows and grows regardless of efforts to stop it, some major belief about the problem or the potential solution is off track. Usually this premise is so basic that we think it cannot be challenged; hence it is paradigm-based. The concept of A.D.D., the beliefs underlying its treatment, and the way other solutions are viewed are excellent examples of paralysis of our current societal (*bodymi*) paradigm.

But there is hope, hope for all of the dedicated teachers and suffering parents who have struggled with our children's education and upbringing. If we inherited this way of thinking, we can change it. Much of what has been proposed in this book is a reversal of what we currently believe. Let's look at attention deficit disorder downside up.

First let's discard the concept of "disorder." Since we accept that children are miracles, we can start there. It is difficult, if not humorous, to think of a miracle being disordered. Remember, everything a child does makes sense, so there is order; we just may not have recognized what it is yet. In fact, the entire world is in astounding order. So, tossing away the word disorder, we are left with two words, *attention* and *deficit.* Where the current paradigm looks for the root of learning problems in physiology (inside the child's body), let's look in a bigger arena. Take *attention* and *deficit* and turn them around. What do you have? A *deficit of attention.*

Could the child's extreme impulsivity or inability to focus be the result of a lack of attention *for* the child, instead of *by* the child? Considering the limitations of our societal mind-set and the singular focus of our educational design, that hypothesis makes perfect sense.

Without passing judgment, let's think about where the child might be lacking attention. One thing I keep in mind is our society's emphasis on the brain. If a child or teen is showing signs of inattentiveness, anxiety, or pent-up energy, the solution more than likely will *not* come from the realm of the brain. If it did, wouldn't we have found it by now? The solution will nearly always come from one of the areas denied by the Bodymi or Knowledge Paradigm.

In seeking solutions, here are some questions I ask myself.

*Are the child's dreams being met?*
Maybe they need more attention. Does the child even know what his or her dreams are?

*Does the child have fears that are causing a need to "run," hence a reason for hyperactivity?*
The solution then becomes giving attention to what is feared and causing the "running." When you move into fear, it disappears. As Franklin Delano Roosevelt said, "The only thing we have to fear is fear itself." Fear motivates you to look and take action. Once you begin to act, the energy from that action becomes a stimulus to continue. By going through the feared action, you make it familiar, so it lacks the unknown quality usually associated

with fear. You are now proud that you acted. Fear is always the predecessor to courage. (Children and teens love that concept, and it works.)

*Are issues of heart not being addressed?*
If so, give attention to the emotional needs of the child.

*Does the child spend time doing what he or she truly loves to do, and is his or her way of "seeing and being" accepted at school and at home?*
Appreciate and give attention to your child's uniqueness. Different is good. Not fitting into the standard way can mean your child has potential beyond the norm. Shouldn't we all long for that? Give attention to what the child loves and desires.

*Are the child's coins invested elsewhere?*
Talk about this with the child. Appreciate the child's uniqueness and nurture it. You might also want to encourage the child to broaden his or her investment. Such a talk is an invitation to lessons on life.

*Is the child shutting off school?*
Has the child perceived a rejection by the school? Remember that any time you feel judged, you sense that judgment as a rejection. Is he or she now rejecting the school, the tasks, or the teacher in return? If so, enlarge on the idea that life is the school. Broaden the arena for success. Give lessons that are reflected in the child's own life. Focus on the power of nonjudgment and the nurturance of dreams.

*Are you an attentive parent, from the child's perspective?*
Are you at home nurturing and loving the child, giving plenty of positive attention? Or are you working loads of hours just to pay the mortgage or rent? Contrary to what you may believe, I have seen hundreds of parents pull back from the work world and spend more time, delightfully, with their children. Such a change can turn the child's life around, make the adult's life more meaningful, and make the family whole again. Don't believe for a minute you cannot move away from your nine-to-five job. Remember that you are here to make life your work, not work your life. Don't wait until the end to find out that owning a house has little to do with success in life. You are your own house. Speaking as someone who used to own a big home with an enormous mortgage, I have learned to live much more simply and happily without being mortgage poor. Our society, with its *bodymi* consciousness, promotes rampant material acquisition that is blatantly disintegrative. Move past the limitation into a larger way of living (maybe in a smaller house).

Let's look at how we might meet the specific needs of a child who seems seriously and habitually inattentive. Remember, of course, we are to seek the "order" or sense, and instead of expecting the child to attend to our design, it is our task to attend to the child's.

The first step in seeking the sense is to look with objectivity. This is a basic concept, but not a simple one. Finding objectivity is not as easy as we might think, especially with our own children. They push our buttons and we push theirs. We all carry our own biases and fears, which we sometimes unknowingly pass on to our children. We are often blind to what is closest to us. To seek the sense through our child's eyes, we often need the assistance of a third party—someone not personally attached to the issues. It is hoped a teacher/educator or counselor will be in this position, but that is not always the case, especially in a time of change when the prevailing attitude or paradigm is challenged. Sandra's Innerwork was designed for this very reason. Everyone working around children *must* do character work or nonjudgmental self-examination, to be as aware of their own issues as possible; otherwise, they can pass them on.

Initially, in seeking the sense, the adult may use nothing more than intuition. As you gain information, the sense becomes clearer. A teacher or counselor's previous experience is of course helpful. A word of caution: don't be attached to a "disability" model. You find what you look for. That is why we say look for the sense.

A prime reason for inattentiveness in a classroom is the child's desire to be attentive to something else. Most often this something else matters more to the child than what the teacher is presenting. (As I said earlier, a child's dreams and emotional realities are more important to the child than any curriculum.) The attention the child is seeking more than likely dwells in the child's life dreams or in the unmet emotional world. If as a teacher I have begun my relationship with each child in my care by eliciting that child's personal dreams, as is recommended in this book, I'm already on the way to understanding where the child's attention may have wandered. If I have informed myself of the emotional realities of my students' lives, then I will have significant information to help me find each child's needs. Now I am ready to begin. My task as the teacher becomes one of connecting with the child's desires in the form of projects and tasks. Because these assignments come out of the child, the child's attention is guaranteed. My next task is to introduce helpful tools and curriculums in the context of the child's dreams.

Let's jump to another way of addressing the attentions of the child previously diagnosed with attention deficit disorder. I have found that a vast majority of hyperactive children have security issues. Considering that our cities are rampant with drugs, crime, homeless people, gangs, and much more, fear makes sense. The fast-paced, heartless world surrounding our children is scary. As I mentioned earlier, those who fear the world at a young age and choose to be extroverted in their response will protect themselves by "running." Running in this case means moving fast literally, and usually includes loving things that move fast—sports, cars, airplanes, spaceships, and computer games. It also means moving fast figuratively, by thinking fast, being funny, and changing the subject often, so as not to get "hit." Males use this defense mechanism more often than do females, and my experience shows that males are more often labeled with A.D.D. Introverts, usually but not exclusively female, who fear the world around them choose to be safe by being quiet and taking refuge inside themselves. This behavior doesn't attract attention like the outwardly moving males'. Such lack of attention is all too often a double-edged sword. Introverts are less likely to get the negative label of having A.D.D., but they often go without help because they aren't the squeaky wheels.

As with all defense mechanisms, running usually works, at least on a short-term basis. The problem arises when the defense fails to work in the long run, as all defense mechanisms also tend to do. How do you remove the need for these defenses? You satisfy the need. You give the child balance; you make sure it is safe for the child to stay put. You surround the child with adults who are clearly concerned for the child above all other things. You place the child in a nonjudgmental environment. You "protect" the child with a few, easy-to-understand rules that do not fluctuate—rules designed to manage behavior, not judge the worth of the child. Archetypally, security is male energy, so one highly effective strategy is to find a male to spend time with the child. (In a society with little male involvement in child rearing, this lack of security again makes sense.)

As teachers or parents, we must learn to use the energy and give it positive direction, rather than dam it and try to force its opposite. If a child says he wants to be a race-car driver, think metaphorically about what the child is telling you. Since metaphor is wide-open, the options become many. Might the child be telling you that he or she wants to move quickly, have fun, be famous, or be a winner? It could certainly be argued that you want a child to learn the opposites of some of those things, but don't fight what the child has (temporarily) chosen. Being fast and fun, first and famous is what our society admires. Many children growing up today have bought this success story. Until you as the adult can model more than this, use this desire! Pick some strategies that create, in a healthy way, the movement, fun, and winning attitude the child is toying with. Make sure the child has plenty of time to play—in and out of school. Remember that play is a wonderful tool we can use to learn about life without judgment.

Help the child learn test facts by playing Bingo with the test answers in the squares. Conduct races on the yard to learn measurement. Have the hyperactive child supervise or be responsible for smaller children at play. Let him be your messenger to other classes, or let her be the class announcer. Use what the child shows you is important, rather than trying to force your own desires. Have the child do something with the class that he or she can shine at doing. Planning to have a hyperactive child sit in a chair for the majority of the day is planning a disaster. Plan activities to get the child out of the chair or, better yet, out of the classroom. Go outside under the trees, or go to the ocean to learn about science. The child will be able to move, learn facts, and practice responsibility at the same time. Whatever you do, make sure to base the activity on the child's dreams and deal with his or her emotional issues before you expect cognitive involvement. It would be truly disordered for a child to attend to reading, spelling, and mathematics while in fear of being unsafe or unloved.

Whether you are a parent or teacher, be creative with what you plan for your naturally creative child. Don't just do what was done with you in school or at home. Remember that our society is upside down. The backward way of thinking being promoted is at the heart of the violence and unrest we see around us. Think and act downside up.

At the Children's Consulting Center, we have traded seeking disability for appreciating the miracle, and judgment for adoration. Robert Frost would be proud. It is the road "less traveled by, and that has made all the difference."

# 10 Adults and Elders

## THE INVITATION

*It doesn't interest me what you do for a living.*

*I want to know what you ache for,*
*And if you dare to dream of meeting your heart's longing.*

*It doesn't interest me how old you are.*

*I want to know if you will risk looking like a fool for love,*
*For your dreams, for the adventure of being alive.*

*It doesn't interest me what planets are squaring your moon.*

*I want to know if you have touched the center of your own sorrow,*
*If you have been opened by life's betrayals or*
*Have become shriveled and closed from fear of further pain!*

*I want to know if you can sit with pain, mine and your own;*
*If you can dance with wildness and let ecstasy fill you*
*To the tips of your fingers and toes without cautioning us to be careful,*
*Be realistic, or to remember the limitations of being human.*

*It doesn't interest me if the story you are telling me is true.*

*I want to know if you can disappoint another to be true to yourself,*
*If you can bear the accusation of betrayal and not betray your own soul.*

*I want to know if you can see beauty*
*Even when it is not pretty every day,*
*And if you can source your life from God's presence.*

*I want to know if you can live with failure, yours and mine,*
*And still stand on the edge of a lake and shout to the silver of the moon, "Yes!"*

*It doesn't interest me to know where you live or how much money you have.*

*I want to know if you can get up after a night of grief and despair,*
*Weary and bruised to the bone, and do what needs to be done for the children.*

*It doesn't interest me who you are, how you came to be here.*

*I want to know if you will stand in the center of the fire with me and not shrink back.*

*It doesn't interest me where or what or whom you have studied.*

*I want to know what sustains you from the inside when all else falls away.*

*I want to know if you can be alone with yourself,*
*And if you truly like the company you keep in the empty moments.*

—Oriah Mountain Dreamer, Native Elder

Most of the strategies in this book focus on the child, since the Center's basic premises are that to be truly effective as parents or educators, we must "begin with the child," and we must utilize strategies that are universally successful with children. But with the welfare of children as our main concern, it makes sense to use adults as the focal point for change.

### Receptive Adults

The strategies presented here that are designed to work with children also work with the child inside each adult. If a parent or adult is receptive to change, ready to move toward wisdom in his or her own life, then one effective approach to help a child change is to use an adult to model the change. The only variable for success is, as always, the receptivity or readiness of the person doing the work. I have learned that by picking the most receptive family member, whether child or parent, change can come about for the whole family.

I often remind parents that children are sponges. They watch and mimic everything we do. Even when you think they aren't watching, they are. For most parents, this mimicking can create funny (and downright embarrassing) moments. But rather than simply cringe when your child repeats one of your less-than-noble expressions, take this concept of mimicry and use it to create strength.

Our children aren't the only ones who must deal with the shallowness of our society. Our children aren't the only ones who have had their dreams squelched or their emotions given a backseat. A child watching parents get on with their lives by pursuing dreams can stimulate movement in the child. Watching Mom get up each morning excited about doing something she truly loves that day has an astounding effect. Watching Dad express tears and fears without hesitation—dealing deeply with life issues instead of ignoring or shunting them—frees the child to do the same. I regularly point out to parents that not just the "identified child" benefits from wise living. Whether the child or the adult seeks happiness, the results are the same.

I cannot count the number of times a parent has come to me wanting a child's life to change, usually seeking counseling for the child—because that is all our old Knowledge Paradigm offers. After thirty minutes into an introduction to the Wisdom Paradigm, with the apparent purpose of getting background for child counseling, the parent begins opening to the emotion and dream work. A tear wells in a mother's eye when I talk about doing what we love. A father sighs and talks about how stressful his high-status, high-paying job is and how he really wanted to design and build wooden furniture. A parent reflects that emotions were never expressed in his or her own family when he or she was a youngster and how painful and insecure that made everyone feel. I usually guide a parent who recognizes this suppression of emotions in his or her family to trace it back as many generations as he or she can. I then invite him or her to be the one to stop it, and to move toward a way of relating that creates more health and happiness.

Many parents I encounter who want to change their children's lives decide to meet with me regularly to get their own lives in gear. How can you change the direction of your child's life unless your own life is focused first? By working with an adult, we can create positive change in an entire family. When one family member learns how to be happy, the happiness becomes contagious. We all want to be happy. We all long to have a full life.

## A Case in Point

Mary came to see me because her son, Nathan, was getting suspended from school. She portrayed him as an angry ten-year-old, diagnosed three years before with attention deficit disorder. He always daydreamed, rarely finished his tasks, and seldom took responsibility for his problems. He could talk his way out of almost any situation, unless he got angry and yelled at the adult. Mary was at the end of her rope. Her son was turned off by school and fought with his mother incessantly over homework. He was no longer respectful of adults, especially his mother. Mary wanted Nathan to receive counseling. He'd been in and out of traditional counseling since he was six years old. Her doctor had recommended that he be medicated so as to increase his attention in class and settle him down. As we talked, it became apparent that her older daughter had problems with depression and sassed her mother as well.

I always premise my work by reminding parents that I am not a counselor, psychologist, or psychiatrist. I am an educator, with decades of experience. Most important, I have learned a different way of approaching children's life problems and education. "Yes," I tell them, "our Center has licensed therapists and certified counselors and teachers, but I might be able to help you collect your own tools to use." I don't usually have to explain, because most of our referrals come from people who have worked with us—a parent, teacher, or counselor familiar with our work and aware of our success record.

In my initial talk with Mary on the phone, I said that if I was successful in our first meeting, she would leave with some ways of creating health and happiness for her son. She indicated that her real purpose was to get him counseling. I explained that there were numerous ways of meeting her son's needs and that one-on-one counseling was only one option. I also told her that our few counseling slots were filled, but that I could refer her elsewhere if, after meeting with me, she still wished to go that direction.

When Mary and I first met, I was struck by how tired she looked. She began by reciting the litany of Nathan's misbehaviors over the years. She brought a folder of test data she had received from the school psychologist that indicated Nathan had a learning disability. We hadn't talked long before I asked one of the usual key questions, "Where is Nathan's father?" Mary sighed and lifted her hands in the air, saying, "He left three and a half years ago." Then she added, "He never was much of a father. Responsibility was always a challenge for him. He's off playing with his adult toys now (cars and motorcycles)."

I listened to Mary, knowing all along that counseling for

Nathan might be helpful, but that if the larger issues of life, love, and security were not addressed as well, the story would remain the same for years to come—changing only in intensity and degree of pain. Experience told me that Nathan was reliving his father's or mother's childhood issues with slightly different wrapping.

I couldn't tell Mary how many thousands of times I had heard this story, with slight variations. A woman was trying to be both father and mother, sole giver of love and affection and sole disciplinarian and provider of security at the same time. The misbehaviors of her children weren't the result of some genetic error of birth. Nathan and his sister were in a story not of their making, scared by and reacting to the trap they perceived they were in. They were confused and afraid. They had life issues that weren't receiving attention, either at home or at school.

As we talked, I began to pull out of Mary the emotions that had been hidden too long. I told her I would take her down into her pain, but that I wouldn't leave her there. I explained that in the depths were more answers. I promised when she left the Center, even after our first talk, she would have *hope* to take along with her. "Money-back guarantee!" I said. She laughed, having already heard that all of our work was for free. "Children are more important than money" was my usual explanation.

After hearing Mary's version of Nathan's story, I had a number of "hits" as to where solutions lay. I showed Mary a design I use to explain the contradiction between the role of the mother and the role of the father and that anyone trying to do both, as million of parents are now forced to do in our society, was in for a rough ride. "How can you love unconditionally, as is the task of all mothers, and give conditional discipline (security), as is the task of all fathers?" This mixed role and mixed message causes children to get anxious and confused, to say the least. "You cannot be successful trying to be the father *and* the mother! But you still have to try." The words sounded contradictory, but I knew the actual solutions would make sense. Mary needed support, as did her children. I explained what a mentorship program was and handed her some application forms. Nathan needed a man to look up to who wouldn't run away. Until his greater needs were at least acknowledged, Nathan's schoolwork would not hold his attention. And Mom needed an occasional break from her children. Mary needed to start following her dream if true change was to occur. She too would be closed to learning new things while the greater issues of life lay hidden under a nine-to-five day. Her job at the insurance company was purely for pay.

Mary easily responded to questions that came from the Wisdom Paradigm. I asked her, "What does Nathan do better than anyone else on earth?" Mary smiled and sat up straight. She dried her cheeks and said confidently, "Nathan can put together anything. He takes apart bicycles, computers, even my vacuum cleaner. Best of all, he can put them back together correctly." I pulled out more aspects of Nathan's talents, showing her how to start with ability rather than disability. It didn't matter what Nathan's gifts were. I was just pointing out that all children have gifts.

Over the next few weeks, I helped Nathan and his

mother plan strategies to focus his energy and attention on his dreams and talents. These strategies would build Nathan up, rather than tear him down. Nathan's problems didn't begin in school, nor did his body create them. He did not need to feel trapped by school or life. He needed the dreams and possibilities that give hope and alleviate anger.

I prodded Nathan's mother to get help from her family, particularly her brother. Nathan needed more male role models, and security obviously was an underlying cause of his anger and his resentful relationship with his mother. Nathan really resented his father for leaving, but in the few times he saw his father, he didn't dare alienate him. So his mother had become the object of his pain, fear, and resentment. I encouraged Mary to have Nathan spend time with his uncle and cousin whenever feasible. Nathan's uncle loved kids and was a natural parent. He would never try to replace Nathan's father, which wasn't his task. He was to show how a healthy man approaches life. He was to protect Mary, Nathan, and Nathan's sister, providing security in any way he could. The uncle's son needed more children around him and Nathan needed a brother figure. All children benefit from play with other children.

Nathan's father showed no sign of wanting to work with the Center. Our overtures to him went ignored, whereas Mary was absolutely mesmerized by our different philosophy. Mary began to schedule weekly meetings with me. Shortly into our second visit, she began to face *her* lost dreams. When I asked her when was the last time someone hugged or protected her, she broke down. I pointed out that the solutions we had talked about for Nathan and his sister were hers, too. With very little probing, I found that Mary had always dreamed of helping others. As a little girl, she daydreamed about being a nurse. She also dreamed of being a mother and understood the immense importance of raising children.

I guided Mary into thinking of ways she could help others and still maintain a job for pay. She came up with options, ranging from volunteering with an agency to setting up a support program for the needy at her church. Since community service is a "universal" for creating health, I pointed out that Nathan or her daughter might want to go with her to serve others.

Mary became the conduit for the change her children needed. She became happier and more patient. She no longer had the whole load of discipline on her shoulders. Her volunteer time gave her a sense of satisfaction and realigned her with the bigger picture of life, which kept her focused on what was truly important. She said "I love you" to her children on a regular basis. Her smile made her face light up, and her tired look was gone. Both children did receive counseling through another agency, but Mary knew enough to find a counselor who was nonjudgmental and in contact with her own bigger picture.

Mary still had days that would challenge her patience and bouts of extreme frustration. Her ex-husband noted a big change in his children's lives but continued to run. Nathan was no longer drawn to his father's way of life. He began working on assembling model cars and learned some computer skills. His future goal was to work in a bicycle shop—for free, of course, until he learned what he needed to know. His mother taught him that. He learned he was safe and comfortable meeting what life brought instead of running from it.

Nathan's self-esteem grew when he saw his own gifts reflected back at him through other people's eyes. He slowly learned to withstand the frustrations he still felt in school. Mary shared some of her ideas with Nathan's teacher, who was encouraged enough to use Nathan's dreams as a basis for his curricular work. Nathan would laugh when his mother called him "beautifully different." He knew those words were another expression of love.

## The Gift of Elders

Let's take this adult focus and shift it one more time. In every community of this country is a vast resource for children we all but ignore, a resource that doesn't cost one cent. This resource is our elders. Elders in many cultures are revered for their wisdom and addressed with titles of honor. We in the industrialized world most often refer to them simply as old people. We mock them for their inability to walk fast, drive with precision, or read clearly—all judgments emanating from a physical consciousness. Our obsession with the *bodymi* causes us to turn away from those whose physical capability is diminishing, though they may have knowledge and compassion. They may understand life far better than any CEO, professional athlete, or Hollywood star. For all but the most hardened, facing mortality creates clarity in all four realms of body, mind, heart, and spirit. Life dreams merge with heart and mind, and we enter the wisdom years.

Elders can be useful in a number of ways. They can come to a classroom to demonstrate a particular art or skill, or they can become classroom aides. They can demonstrate business talent or lead field excursions. One of the most effective ways an elder can help is as a mentor or big brother/sister to one of the many teenagers missing a parent. All children need a mother and father, the archetypal roles of a woman who will love them unconditionally and a man who will guide and protect them.

Back in Chapter 6 we noted the importance of designing teenagers' educational experience on both sides of the lifefence. We returned teens to childhood to revisit where they came from, and we recommended that they spend a portion of the day looking at where they may be heading. If as a teacher you are aware of each child's dream, you can plan, with the help of the children and their parents, visits from people they dream of becoming. You then have twenty instances or so (depending on the size of the class) of an adult coming to a classroom (or a student or class going to an adult's place of work) and the child getting to see and talk with a person living his or her dream. The other kids watch a dream being nurtured, which encourages them to pursue their own dreams even more diligently. Remember here that I am not equating dream with job, though that may be the teenagers' approach. A number of doctors, business executives, lawyers, pilots, and accountants who have done very well in their field now want to return something to society in another way. The same is

Many years ago my in-laws invited a less-than-favorite grandfather to a family dinner. He was over ninety years old and living under the supervision of one of his grandchildren in the back cottage. He could be left on his own, as he often was, but conscience won out for the evening. His granddaughter brought him to the gathering as a kind of duty. His eyes were rheumy, his massive back was stooped, and he couldn't hear well, but you could tell he must have been a formidable figure in his younger years. According to the stories I was told, he was quite a brute as a young man and a father. He was known for his quick judgment of others, and for his borderline cruelty to his wives (he had outlived two) and children. As karma would have it, he was now being judged, as he had judged.

But I wasn't part of this family's early story. I didn't know personally the pain of his backhand or tongue. All I saw was a gentle hulk of a man with blue peeking out from behind the clouds in his eyes. I looked at his hands—the biggest hands I had ever seen—and saw lifetimes in the calluses and creases. If you spoke loudly and directly in one ear, he could hear you—a lot more clearly than others gave him credit for. In fact, inside his deteriorating body was an alert mind, resigned to sitting in its own world but eager to be drawn out. Since I was the only one who would speak much to him, he was delighted when I sat near. While the others went on about their socializing, seemingly oblivious to his presence, I pulled stories out of this man. He had spent most of his life on a farm in "Ioway." He told me of working the soil, growing corn, and fighting insects with such clarity that I could smell the moist humus and hear the incessant buzzing of the locust. He passed on to me a recipe for dandelion wine that he took pride in. He had volumes of tales that, in all likelihood, would be lost soon—and lost forever.

There was a kindergartner still inside this man. There was an explanation for his pain and anger. There were lessons his family needed to understand, so as not to repeat his mistakes. By ignoring this man, by ignoring his physical presence, they were ignoring his life "presents." ●

true for singers, dancers, martial art masters, and composers. You may even find a "slam poet," a motorcycle racer, or a bird caller. They may not be earning money doing what they love. What matters is that they are fulfilling their dreams.

Just as teenagers are being encouraged in schools to serve the community, adults are finding the same sense of satisfaction in serving others. Many businesses today encourage employees to give a set number of hours back to the community. Some businesses are participating in adopt-a-school programs. Parents whose children are grown may enjoy having "kid energy" around. Adults who never had children because they were pursuing careers may like to slow down and experience raising a child, in a limited fashion. I have run into numerous adults who feel grateful for the lives they have led and want to give back to the community. Take what comes your way and use it to benefit the children.

I will add a point of caution. We want healthy adults as role models for our children. Just as we need to be aware of whom we send into a classroom as a teacher or a classroom aide, we need to screen adults volunteering in mentor relationships. But our fear can serve to keep us alert, not stop us from acting. Big Brothers and Big Sisters of America have been successfully pairing adults and children for decades; their screening process is well honed. Other well-established organizations, such as Families for Youth and Building Futures (a subgroup of YMCA), also screen thoroughly and prepare the adults for mentoring. The universals for teachers discussed in Chapter 8 also apply to mentors and adults spending time in the classroom. They must love life and children, work always with the children's welfare in mind, seek to be nonjudgmental, and be aware of their own potentially unprocessed "ego" issues.

### Another Case in Point

The mentorships our Center sponsors require a high level of responsibility. We have kids who need more than a parent figure, kids who have experienced life trauma most of us only read about. We choose our matches slowly and carefully, talking to the mentor, parent, and child all along the way. If we create a match, great. If not, fine. Under no circumstances do we want to create an uneven match. All three key figures—child, parent, and mentor—have to bond.

Theresa is an active member of her community. She has held numerous PTA offices and positions on many city and county committees. Theresa is a pleasure to be with. She loves life and appreciates its gifts and blessings. She has also experienced pain, losing loved ones and going through financial troubles. Yet she has tried to grow from whatever life has sent her way.

Theresa and her husband raised two stalwart boys. One has a family and his own real estate business; the other lives in Europe with his wife. Theresa loved being a mother (not that the job is ever done). She came to me as so many do, intrigued by stories of our Center. The conversation usually starts with "What is it that you do? I've heard some good things but I'm not sure I understand." So begins a conversation on educating children and stopping societal violence at the same time.

"How can I help?" Theresa asked.

I gave her a number of suggestions and described different roles and levels of participation. When I described the need for big sisters, her eyes lit up.

"I love my boys dearly, but I always wanted a daughter, too. Maybe I could be a grandmother to a young girl for a few months."

I told Theresa to go home and think about our conversation. I asked her to call me in a few days.

Theresa left with a huge smile on her face. A few minutes went by, and the phone rang. Theresa was calling on a cell phone. She wanted to tell me she had thought long enough. "When can I begin the training?"

I met with Theresa a couple of times before I found a child to match with her. I asked Kate and Wendy, two of our counselors, for suggestions for matches. The counselor is key not only in selecting the mentor, but also in supervising the mentorship relationship over the three-month period we usually start with.

James is a carpenter. His daughter, Cerise, is the love of his life. And James does love life, because he has been diagnosed with a life-threatening illness. He is a good man who made some bad choices in his earlier years. He and his wife had a lot of fun—at least for a while—with drink and drugs. One day he woke up, in more ways than one, stopped drinking, and began the long journey back. His wife moved on to harder stuff and one day disappeared, leaving James and Cerise to fend for themselves.

That was three years ago. Cerise is now eight years old. She misses her mother dearly and resents her at the same time. Cerise is very bright—a brightness that comes from having your eyes opened wide very early in life. Nothing scares her anymore—except maybe losing her father. Cerise has the intensity of a child who has already known great pain and lives fully as a result. She can be loud and passionate, loving and troublesome. Whatever she does, she does it with gusto.

After meeting with James and broaching the idea of a big sister, I waited for him to discuss it with Cerise. I contacted Theresa to say I had a potential child and asked her to come in and talk with me. Theresa came in excited and a little nervous. (We know how children fear rejection, but we forget that adults fear it, too.)

I scared Theresa with Cerise's story. She cried, and then worried about whether she was prepared for this little girl. I asked her if she could love a child and accept the pain of losing her one day. She hesitated.

"Yes," she said. She knew a little girl needed her.

I've only had a couple of mentorships go awry. When they do, it is usually because the adult becomes sidetracked and pulls away—a disaster for the child. This one didn't go wrong. Cerise, James, and Theresa became a powerful trio. Cerise couldn't get enough of Theresa. James gained a wise elder, a woman to ask questions of. And Theresa got the daughter she had always longed for.

The relationship, for the first three-month period, was kept formal and regimented. Theresa began by seeing Cerise on a set schedule, checking with James to see when and where to pick her up for excursions to the library or the mall. Buying things for kids is not part of our mentoring program, but the two of them would walk through the mall arm in arm, dreaming of houses, clothes, and life in general. Theresa also helped with homework and answered the little girl's questions about sexuality. Cerise's quarter report card was quite impressive. At the end of the three months, James, Theresa, Cerise, and their counselor all agreed the relationship should be extended. I carefully talked with Theresa to make sure she knew where the relationship was going. She knew.

Cerise and Theresa developed a strong relationship. Cerise tried a few times to alienate Theresa to see if she would run like her mother did, but Theresa stood firm. Theresa took an extended vacation in the middle of the second three months, but she and Cerise exchanged letters, and Cerise learned that people do return.

Who knows what the future has in store for Cerise, James, or Theresa. But one thing is certain: their lives were changed by simple human kindness. Theresa took a risk and spent time with a little girl. She talked to and listened to her with her heart. James got help and companionship during an important time in his daughter's life. Cerise learned to love and be loved by a woman.

Caroline Myss said (and I paraphrase) it sometimes doesn't matter much what decisions we make; what matters absolutely is the intention with which we make them. Bring adults with good intentions to children and miracles will happen. They need not be experts. They need not have credentials or certification. They need not be perfect; they may hesitate to act because they are afraid of failure or of not being good enough. All they need is to get past their "selves" and come to children with the children's true well-being in mind . . . unattached to how that well-being may manifest itself.

Elders have been there. Parents have lived longer than their children. Yes, they have had more time to make mistakes. They may have been seriously callous or blind in their early life pursuits, but something happens when you reach your wisdom years. Something happens when you pass the midpoint and begin to look at your own mortality.

I am reminded of the story of the poor, wandering man who is in need of food and clothing. He has spent the last ten years alone on the backroads of life, wandering away from other people's expectations. As he walks along the street looking for cigarette butts, he comes upon a bag of silver dollars lying in the path in front of him. Not seeing what's inside, he kicks the bag away and mumbles proudly to himself how alert he is to see this bag and kick it aside before he tripped.

We are all surrounded by "bags of silver." They are everywhere. All we need to do is remember how clear things were in our kindergarten years and heed Fulghum's recommendation and—LOOK.

# 11 A Wise and Healthy Classroom

*Kids go where there is excitement.*
*They stay where there is love.*
—Zig Ziglar

Many people, upon hearing of the Wisdom Paradigm, or of another way to educate children, ask for a step-by-step process to change from the old to the new. Parents and teachers alike want a list of what to do and when to do it. That is how we have done things in the past, but that way lacks a key component. To refer back to Einstein's wisdom, we must alter our underlying belief system to create actual change. I am reminded of what my tai chi teacher says about people who know the steps in a tai chi routine but don't have the feel of the chi: they are copying the movements without understanding the soul of the art. Since the Wisdom Paradigm begins in the spirit and heart realms, it must be founded there, not in the mind. If people understand the basic beliefs of the Wisdom Paradigm, they can design their own classroom or school.

I recommend starting with the universals from Chapter 8, and most specifically with one of the hardest—*seeking to see or interact with children without judgment.* If teachers were to pick this universal and attempt to implement it, they would be well on their way to a revolutionary change.

Seeking to be nonjudgmental sounds simple enough. But not only is it one of the most critical components of this design based on the Wisdom Paradigm, it is one of the most challenging. To get a taste of how difficult this shift can be, go through an entire day holding the concept of judgment in the forefront of your thoughts. Carry a pad of paper and pen or a tape recorder, and record every time you find yourself judging a person or thing (even if it's only in your thoughts). I think you'll be amazed at how quickly judgment rises. Remember that the Knowledge Paradigm, which underlies our current societal mind-set and our educational system, is built on judgment. To be judgmental is part of being human, and transcending it is key to seeking wisdom.

Anthony Robbins explains that we must stop thinking in terms of success and failure, and think instead in terms of results or outcomes. Don't stop and judge what happens; simply learn from the results of what happens and move forward. This is how we must teach our children, and this is what we must do in our own lives first.

If you are an educator working in a traditional public or private school, start with small changes. Grading a child's work is the most pervasive form of judgment. Correcting a paper is different from grading a paper. In many cases, correcting is necessary for learning to take place, but the correcting must be done out of the mutual pursuit of learning, not out of a need to grade or judge. You may not be able to stop grading papers right away, but maybe in the

*CILS, not only the school itself, but the students and the teachers, made me feel like I wasn't an outcast anymore. I found out the teacher and my classmates really cared for me when I went to juvenile hall. They sent me a couple of letters, and my mom doesn't even do that. CILS made a lot of changes in me, all good, my attitude towards people and my life. It also made me change the way I deal with my problems. I think this small school setting is a great way to deal with problems. I think this small classroom setting is a great way to teach and help kids. CILS is supposed to be a school for education, but I think of it as a lesson for life.* —**R.**

not-so-distant future you could pilot (model) a different way. Offer grades for those who feel that grades help them learn, and model something different for those who feel the burn of judgment underlying the grades. Set up portfolios for the children. Have them select pieces of work that they feel represent their current level of work and place them in the folders. Begin with pride and excitement for each child's choice. As the days or weeks progress, have the children select additional pieces of work that they think show their growth, and place them next in the file. Eventually each child will have a large file to display months of work and months of growth. Emphasize growth and the pursuit of knowledge, not a finite attainment level. Letting children choose projects to work on and move to completion is one of the most effective methods of educating. Students then have finished projects to exhibit and take pride in. This positive way of displaying and taking pride in work feels good to children and demonstrates growth in a way that grades do not. The success of this nonjudgmental approach will attract those who previously settled for grades.

To create a school or classroom under the wisdom design, simply start from where you are. I had the fortune to start from scratch, with some dynamic coworkers, to build a mini-school for troubled teens. However, we were able to do that within the existing system only because we took on kids no one else wanted to deal with. With the support of the superintendent (whose trust was based in part on my nearly thirty years of experience in education), the teachers and I had free rein. This is by far the best way to start, but most teachers or principals I work with look at me with frustration because they are more bound to the larger educational system.

Let's look at some simple steps that can be taken to set up a wiser classroom, taking for granted that you understand the philosophy of the Wisdom Paradigm. These steps may look simple, but implementing them will take determination and clarity. Once you start putting the pieces in place, and you experience the increased level of success, you will be motivated to continue.

- Begin each day by meeting the children as they come off the bus or first arrive on campus. Greet each one with a touch or a look, a welcome on the spiritual level. Deepak Chopra tells us that *namaste*, the traditional Hindu greeting, does just this. Loosely translated, namaste means "The spirit in me sees the spirit in you and I meet you there." After visiting schools in Japan, I came back with a number of ideas I wanted to implement in my own school. Many schools there had official greeters, children who bowed and welcomed each child entering school. The bow and the words conveyed a level of honor and respect uncommon in the United States. When I returned to San Mateo, I decided to stand at a main entrance of the elementary school and welcome, in honor, each person, the children in particular. I tried to touch children's shoulders or make eye contact, especially with children who had had a discipline problem the previous day. I greeted them with a delight for life and love for children.

End each day in a similar fashion. I watched a teacher in our district, Sheila McQuade, dismiss her students one by one by touching their shoulders, looking them in the eye, and reminding them of something special that happened that day. No child left unacknowledged. "Michael, what a delightful map you drew today. Laticia, you were so helpful to others today. Marcia, you made my day with your smile. Johnny, what was your favorite part of this day?" Johnny thought for a moment, then said, "You know how much I like music. I liked the music we made today."

- A classroom with four walls is part of the old educational design. Instead, I like to think of the classroom as home base or home ground. Learning takes place regularly in other rooms and outside, in nature and in the community. Angeles Arrien says that to be healthy, a person must be in nature one hour a day, minimum. Use nature to create health, for your children and yourself. Walk in the schoolyard studying trees or insects. Collect leaves for art projects. Teach children not to fear the elements. Encourage their natural delight and show the order all around you. Study nature's cycles. Watch butterflies emerge, rain fall, or ice form on puddles. Walk down the street to look at the neighborhood, visit stores, or sing in retirement homes. Nothing I am suggesting here is new. Kindergarten teachers have done all of these things. If you are studying the ocean, go to the ocean. If you are studying mathematics, examine the order of nature. If you are studying history, go to historical sites. In the old educational design, field trips were a reward at the end of the year. Make them a daily reward, and appreciate being alive.

- Teachers should have a clear concept of the life dreams and the emotional issues of each and every child in their care (just as kindergarten teachers do). Drawing out this information should be a prime task at the beginning of the school year. Do it nonjudgmentally, showing the children trust and honor. Your success will be determined by your awareness of their issues and your nurturing of their dreams. The teacher/student relationship is one of the most important relationships in life—for both participants.

- As children approach the school in the morning, look carefully at their faces and notice their energy. Be aware of potential emotional issues. If someone is angry or sad, gently pull the child aside and invite him or her to talk for a moment. Catching anger, depression, or fear before a student enters the classroom can stave off a collision. Remember that learning that comes from our emotions is more important than any curriculum. Take advantage of this opportunity. Find and use the life lessons underlying the pain. Have the child go sit with a good listener. Make sure the child knows you are not ignoring the underlying issues. Your relationship work will come back to help you here.
- Do not be afraid to touch children. Without touch, we become unhealthy. Of course, touch needs to be appropriate, and you have to keep in mind children's past issues of abuse or neglect. Teenage boys like to be bumped, patted on the shoulder, or given a thumbs-up. With trust, camaraderie, and practice, hugging can become the norm with any age.
- The classroom atmosphere should be multisensory. Play music and videos. Keep plants and animals in the room; a dog or cat can have an amazing impact. Use

soft lighting at the beginning of the day and at other appropriate times. Stimulate all of the senses, not just those of the *bodymi*.

- Take full advantage of the technological revolution. One reason for the Wisdom Paradigm's rise is the astounding level of communication—the narrowing of the world—that comes from the computer world. Technology offers amazing tools to promote learning and connect us with people and information all over the world.

- Have children and staff participate in keeping the school and grounds clean. This work creates a sense of order and responsibility. Children may also grow and prepare their own lunches. The practice is common in Japan and is already operational in a few schools in the United States.

- Let's return song and dance to our children and teens. When working with groups of adults who were processing childhood issues, Angeles Arrien would ask two questions, "When did you stop singing?" and "When did you stop dancing?"

- Do the same task first every day. Regimen and simple rules make children and teens feel secure.

- When misbehavior arises—as it is supposed to—use the event as a life lesson. Remember to discipline the behavior, not the child. Set up clear rules and expectations. Many children today come to school with issues of insecurity. Security is more important than academics. Not addressing these issues will severely stifle cognitive learning. Use words and behaviors that show children they are safe.

- With older students, make writing in their personal journals the first task of the day. They can reflect on questions that delve into the spirit or heart realm. One example would be, "Think of an important adult in your life—a parent, a brother or sister, a grandparent, or someone else special. What do you think they wanted to be when they were your age? Do you think they fulfilled their life dream? If so, how? If not, do you think they could do it now? What do you think *their* parent's life dream was? Do you know if he or she fulfilled that dream?" (Books with these kinds of questions are usually sold under the heading "character development.") These questions must not have right or wrong answers, nor should any of the writing be graded. These journals are for the students, and for the teacher to read later, to create understanding and relationship. Never judge. Such acceptance is key to the teacher/child relationship.
- Never forget that education comes from the child and that the learner's desire to learn is the most critical factor for retaining learning. All curriculums must be presented within the context of this desire. Begin with the child's dreams and desires. Treat curriculums as tools to meet the child's pursuit.

- Invite to class other teachers (elders, tradespeople, specialists) whose work reflects the life dreams of a certain child, or let the child go to them. Other children may observe or participate, so they can see someone chase his or her dream; eventually everyone gets a turn.

- Have both a male and a female adult in the classroom. This shared leadership is critical to children's development for many reasons. The universe is ordered in yin and yang. Ignoring this is folly. On a more practical level, having both a male and a female adult in the classroom gives children the opportunity to work out their father or mother "issues" and do basic relationship work. Many, if not most, children come to school from one-parent homes or from homes where one or both parents are pulled away from their children due to the pressures of work. Schools can help with this vacuum until our society balances itself. Staffing schools in today's world is difficult, so you may think I am asking for the impossible. But I believe people will become attracted to education because of the new design's effectiveness. They will also be drawn to the awesome level of service inherent in wisdom education; pay, in the form of money, will be secondary. The pay under the wisdom design comes in many forms: hugs, thanks, letters of gratitude. They motivate you, keep you on track, and in fact make you stronger each day. The current lack of respect for educators in our society is a result of our education system's shallow design and mixed success. Depth of teaching and depth of responsibility engender respect. The work done daily in the wisdom design affects teachers as well as students. The universals and the four realms of being human are key to life, not just to education. If you follow your path, money will come. If you follow your path, security will come. If you follow your path, all that you need will come.

- Optimal class size should be appropriate to the needs of the children, not mandated by law or as a reaction to funding. Our alternative school/classroom never exceeded fourteen youth, with two adult supervisors. Money, politics, and mandates have no place in determining class size. As educators, we must plan what is needed for our children, begin to implement the plan, and then find funding. Even if funding is limited, education need not be.
- Use portfolios, as recommended above. These collections of work display progress without judgment.
- Have older children and teens spend at least one hour a day working with younger children, preferably during the morning. Carefully choose, nurture, and supervise these child-teen relationships.
- Make service to others a regular component of the educational program. Community service moves children out of ego to a consciousness of "all," which is critical to both the health of the individual and the health of the society as a whole.

- Let's learn from the old one-room schoolhouse. Obviously the enclosed one-room concept is limiting, but structuring education so that children of all ages, in community, learn together is a good idea. Even though we know that all six-year-olds aren't the same, we're used to the age-level groupings of the old educational design. We need to transcend simple numerical measures and create family learning environments.
- Homework is supposed to create a sense of responsibility and connect the education of the school with the home. It succeeds partially, by connecting all that is upside down in our educational design with the home. But what if we designed homework to be a delight? What if it strengthened family relationships? What if children couldn't wait to get back to school the next day to share what they had done? What if the return work helped reduce the teacher's workload the following day? The wisdom design applies to homework, too. I have decided to devote an entire book to this one change, which is another way of introducing the Wisdom Paradigm.

What ideas can you come up with? Use your heart and mind, your own inherent wisdom, to create your design. Each chapter of this book presents key concepts to keep in mind. Let the four realms, the universals, and the redefinition of education be your guide. Better yet, let the children tell you what to do.

# Conclusion

*No more turning away*
*From the weak and the weary*
*No more turning away*
*From the coldness inside*
*Just a world that we all must share*
*It's not enough just to stand and stare*
*Is it only a dream that there'll be*
*No more turning away?*

—D. Gilmour and A. Moore, "On the Turning Away,"
© 1987 Pink Floyd Music Publishers, Inc.

In turning toward a new world and toward peace, the steps are clear. We will need determination, stamina, and perseverance to complete the changes, and a more developed sense of consciousness as well. But the steps are not only doable—they are more than likely a part of our destiny. Like the child who needs to test limits to find out what will hurt, we as a human species have been testing incredible boundaries, hopefully coming away with knowledge that will bring us closer to a truly healthy world.

A well-accepted concept in philosophy states that we feel the most disruption, fear, and stress just before a major change occurs. The degree of pain is in direct proportion to the degree of change. For us to shift to what could be an Age of Wisdom, it has taken the horrors of a half-century of worldwide war, culminating in the Holocaust and the bombings of Hiroshima and Nagasaki. These extremes of inhumanity are bringing about change the likes of which we have never seen. We have been oblivious of the change because we are in the change itself. This renaissance will be not of artistic expression but of wisdom itself. It will be a leaving of the patriarchal and warring consciousness, and a return, with a greater understanding, to a world that honors both our feminine and masculine natures.

In the name of the next generation, I offer the following points of summary in the hope that there will be no more turning away.

- Massive change must be systemic. Systemic change comes about only by challenging the paradigms of thought that are no longer functional. Our entire society, including our educational, political, economic, medical, and social systems, is based on a paradigm that is now dysfunctional. It underlies our society's ill health.
- Massive change comes about by focusing on children, and implementing solutions that will help us raise the next generation differently.
- Teachers, parents, and seekers of change cannot get into every household, but we can get into (nearly) every classroom. Our educational system can be the vehicle of change. A peaceful revolution of our existing educational mind-set can be the answer we are all seeking.

- To be healthy, happy, and fulfilled as individuals and as a society, we must fully explore all four realms of our humanity: the material, psychological, emotional, and spiritual (body, mind, heart, and spirit).
- Our society's current mind-set is made up of the material (body) and a small portion of the psychological (mind) worlds. I refer to this paradigm as the *bodymi*. It excludes and denies the larger realms of mind, heart, and spirit.
- Killings such as those that have been plaguing our country recently are a direct result of the removal of the heart and spirit components from our society and its systems. One way to help stop the killings is to systematically reinstate these realms in our homes, our schools, and our communities.
- Everything a child (or any person) does makes sense. By seeking the sense, you open yourself and your child up to answers and possibilities.
- In parenting, teaching, or counseling, your task is to see the sense through the child's eyes, without judgment.
- Judgment stops learning. Nonjudgment facilitates it.
- Children thrive on love, security, and nonjudgment. We need to raise and educate them with depth, compassion, and a bigger perspective on what it means to be alive.

- Education is both an inner study and an outer study. It is the pursuit of "Who am I?" and "What is this world around me?"
- To become educated is to prepare yourself for life, not simply a job. Education for the pursuit of a job is a limited, temporary pursuit.
- Education is a process, not the seeking of an end. Measuring finite points (grading) actually stops learning.
- Reading, writing, and arithmetic are tools or skills to be learned in the context of something else. The something else is the person's life dreams.
- All children (people) have life dreams. Pursuing life dreams is where learning begins.
- The most effective educational design begins with the child's life dreams (spirit), then moves to issues of emotion (heart), and then to the huge realm of mind, and last to the important area of body. Effective learning moves smoothly in a circle, exploring all four realms.
- Nature, music, art, dance, play, and fantasy are but a few of the critical components for the health and education of a child, an adult, and a society. We have downplayed or ignored these things in our schools for too long.
- Master teachers possess certain universal traits. These universals include, but are not limited to, a love of chil-

dren, a love of learning, an ability to be nonjudgmental, and an ability to make children feel secure.

This book attempts to describe how we can increase the effectiveness of education while stopping the landslide of disintegration and violence in our society. Solutions to the first problem provide solutions to the second. True education—education that studies the full range of human experience—reduces violence and alienation by giving meaning and hope where there has been none.

*The breeze at dawn has secrets to tell you.*
*Don't go back to sleep!*
*You must ask for what you really want.*
*Don't go back to sleep!*
*People are going back and forth across the doorsill*
*where the two worlds touch.*
*The door is round and open. Don't go back to sleep!*

—Rumi, "Across the Doorsill"

# Bibliography


Arrien, Angeles. *The Four-Fold Way.* San Francisco: Harper San Francisco, 1993.

Barker, Joel E., and Ray J. Christenson. *The Business of Paradigms* (video recording). Burnsville, Minnesota: Charthouse Learning Corporation, 1989.

Bloom, Benjamin S., Bertram B. Mesia, and David R. Krathwohl. *Taxonomy of Educational Objectives.* New York: David McKay, 1964.

Breton, Denise, and Christopher Largent. *The Paradigm Conspiracy.* Center City, Minnesota: Hazelden, 1996.

Brussat, Frederic, and Mary Ann Brussat. *Spiritual Literacy.* New York: Simon & Schuster, Inc., 1998.

Canfield, Jack, and Mark Victor Hansen. *Chicken Soup for the Soul.* Deerfield Beach, Florida: Health Communications, 1993.

Carter-Scott, Cherie. *If Life Is a Game, These Are the Rules.* New York: Bantam Doubleday Dell Publishing Group, 1998.

Chopra, Deepak. *Ageless Mind, Timeless Body.* New York: Crown Publishers, Inc., 1993.

———. *Synchrodestiny* (audio set). Niles, Illinois: Nightingale Conant Corp., 1998.

Chopra, Deepak, and David Simon. *Training the Mind, Healing the Body* (audio book). Niles, Illinois: Nightingale Conant, 1997.

Covey, Stephen R., and A. Roger and Rebecca R. Merrill. *First Things First* (audio book). New York: Simon & Schuster, Inc., 1994.

Ferrucci, Piero. *Inevitable Grace: Breakthroughs in the Lives of Great Men and Women: Guides to Your Self-Realization.* Translated by David Kennard. A Jeremy P. Tarcher/Putnam Book. New York: G. P. Putnam's Sons, 1990.

Fox, Matthew. *The Reinvention of Work.* New York: HarperCollins Publishers, 1995.

## bibliography

Frankl, Victor. *Man's Search for Meaning.* New York: Simon & Schuster, Inc., 1984.

Froebel, Friedrich. *The Education of Man.* Translated from the German and annotated by W. N. Hailmann. New York: August M. Kelley Publishers, 1970. First published 1885.

Fromm, Erich. *To Have or to Be?* New York: Continuum Publishing Company, 1999.

Fulghum, Robert. "All I Really Need to Know I Learned in Kindergarten." In *Uncommon Thoughts on Common Things.* New York: Villard Books, 1988.

Gaarder, Jostein. *Sophie's World.* New York: Berkley Books, 1996.

Gandhi, Mohandas K. *Gandhi, an Autobiography.* Boston: Beacon Press, 1957.

Gatto, John Taylor. *Dumbing Us Down.* Philadelphia: New Society Publishers, 1999.

Goethe, Johann Wolfgang von. *Goethe's Way of Science: A Phenomenology of Nature.* SUNY Series in the Environment and Architectural Phenomenology. Introduction by David Seamon and preface by Arthur Zajonc. New York: State University of New York, 1998.

Hammarskjold, Dag. *Markings.* Toronto: Ballantine Books, 1993.

Hillman, James. *The Soul's Code: In Search of Character and Calling.* New York: Random House, 1996.

Hoffer, Eric. *The True Believer: Thoughts on the Nature of Mass Movements.* New York: Harper, 1951.

Hubbard, Barbara Marx. *Conscious Evolution.* Novato, California: New World Library, 1998.

Karns, Michelle. *The Trick Bag.* Sebastopol, California: National Training Associates, 1993.

Krishnamurti, J. *Education and the Significance of Life.* New York: Harper Collins Publishers, 1981.

Kuhn, Thomas. *The Structure of Scientific Revolutions.* Chicago: University of Chicago Press, 1962.

Merton, Thomas. *Gandhi on Non-Violence.* New York: New Directions Publishing, 1965.

Meyers, Isabel Briggs, and Peter B. Meyers. *Gifts Differing: Understanding Personality Type.* Palo Alto, California: Davies-Black Publishing, 1995.

## bibliography

Myss, Caroline. *Anatomy of the Spirit.* New York: Crown Publishers, 1996.

Pais, Abraham. *"Subtle is the Lord . . .": The Science and the Life of Albert Einstein.* New York: Oxford University Press, 1982.

Palmer, Helen. *The Enneagram: Understanding Yourself and Others in Your Life.* San Francisco: Harper San Francisco, 1991.

Palmer, Parker J. *The Courage to Teach.* San Francisco: Jossey-Bass, 1998.

Quinn, Daniel. *Ishmael.* New York: Bantam Books, 1992.

——. *The Story of B.* New York: Bantam Books, 1996.

Riso, Don Richard. *Personality Types.* Boston: Houghton Mifflin Company, 1987.

Robbins, Anthony, and Frederick L. CoVan. *Awaken the Giant Within: How to Take Immediate Control of Your Mental, Emotional, Physical and Financial Destiny!* New York: Summit Books, 1991.

Siegel, Bernie. *Out of My Mind* (audio book). Berkeley, California: New Medicine Tapes, 1997.

Tarnas, Richard. *The Passion of the Western Mind.* New York: Crown Publishers, 1991.

Walters, J. Donald. *Education for Life.* Nevada City, California: Crystal Clarity, 1997.

Zajonc, Arthur. *The New Hephaestus: The Sacred Dimension of Technology* (audio set). For the California Institute of Integral Studies series "Towards a New World View" with Professor Richard Tornas. San Francisco: Conference Recording Service, TNW, 1996.

Zukav, Gary. *The Seat of the Soul.* New York: Simon and Schuster, 1989.

# Acknowledgments

To all who came before me, who gave of their lives selflessly so that my path would be clearer, especially my mother and father.

To all of the children who have died so that we might see, and the parents who still mourn, you will not be forgotten.

To all of the educators who give of themselves daily to the children of this country and who work so hard to try to create a healthy future generation, know you are appreciated, and have hope.

To those good people who doubt, resist change, and continue to toil, attached to the old educational system regardless of outcomes, I am forever thankful. By learning not to judge you, by watching carefully what was not working, I was able to see clearly the dire need for change, what to change, and how to change it.

To Margene Janzen, who stuck with me through all others' doubt, hesitation, and fear; who gave of her time, her expertise, and her ideas with little or no pay; who allowed me to vent, try new ideas, fail, and reach for the stars. The children and I will forever be grateful. Without your unwavering support, I'm not sure these ideas would have ever reached print.

To my dear, loving wife, who had to live with me day and night no matter what hurdle I was trying to jump, and who now opens to whatever steps remain—thank you for your patience. I love you!

To Sandra Larragoiti, dear friend and comrade, I am forever in your debt for having awoken the tiger inside of me and then given the tiger the wisdom to walk gently. Your words ring throughout this book.

To the staff at the Center, whose task has been, and continues to be, to dive daily with true responsibility into any and all problems of children, families, and education. After all the smoke has cleared, you are still standing. I am so proud of you!

To Susan Sneller, who was the first person to read this book's original thirty chapters and bravely recommended a reduction and restructuring of my work. Thank you for your professional expertise. To Melody Lacina, who worked with me word by word, torturous cut by cut, and who fortuitously recommended and guided me through a major format change, I appreciate all you have done. To Christine Taylor and the other professionals at Wilsted & Taylor Publishing Services, your creativity, professional advice, and sensibility were invaluable.

And to all of those who rise each day determined to make the world a better place, have hope: change is on the wind.

# No More Turning Away

**A Revolution in Education / Solutions for a Violent World**

______ copies at $17.95 each = ______

**Sales tax and handling:**

**Add 8% sales tax ($1.44) per book if shipped to California address** ______

**Priority 2-day mail $4.00 (first book); add $2.00 each additional** ______

**Total** ______

**Send check and order form to:** **Education4YourLife**
**P.O. Box 25298**
**San Mateo, CA 94403**

**Ship to:**

**Name** ______________________________

**Address** ______________________________

**City** ____________________ **State** ______ **Zip** ______

Mr. Veronda is available as an inspirational speaker
or workshop presenter to groups wishing to create change.
He can be reached at (650) 654-7934.

Audio tapes available soon: *www.Education4YourLife.org*

Communication welcome. Send all comments or discussion to
*ronveronda@netscape.net*

**Please help spread the word about this book and the paradigm shift it proposes.**

Donations gratefully accepted.
If you would like to contribute to the work of finding and spreading *true solutions* to the problems of children, please send donations to the address above. Proceeds will be used to make the world a better place for the next generation. Help make the world a better place because *you* were here.